SHEDDING LIGHT ON THE HOLLYWOOD BLACKLIST:
Conversations with Participants

by
Stanley Dyrector

BearManor
Media

Albany, Georgia

Published in the USA by:
BearManor Media
P.O. Box 1129
Duncan, OK 73534-1129
www.BearManorMedia.com

ISBN-10: 1-59393-244-8
ISBN-13: 978-1-59393-244-2

Editors: Wes Britton and Michael Schemaille

Design and layout by Allan T. Duffin

Printed in the United States of America

To My Wife, Joyce

Table of Contents

Acknowledgements

This book never would have happened without the prior sacrifices for freedom of speech and expression that my uniquely talented guests endured. If I could speak to each of them today, I would thank them once again for their contributions. They had great patience, sympathy, and understanding in participating with me, a naïve wild card. It must have been difficult to delve back into a past that had filled their lives with angst, turmoil, and uncertainty as their destinies were suspended by continuing victimization, with families torn apart, some never to mend. Through the years when I did my cable TV show, there were many people whose expertise and generous assistance were vital to our success. I hasten to add that a complete list of those who helped would be too long to include here. Nevertheless I thank them and take pride in the fact that our three programs with Four

Blacklistees, won Wave Awards from the Alliance for Community Media.

For my more prosaic efforts, I must give special thanks to Writers Guild of America/West Foundation Librarian, Karen Pederson, and Angela Kirgo, Executive Director of the Foundation for their invaluable assistance in tracking down often obscure historical data.

Foreword by Ed Asner

I have often felt that only one, or at most two, blacklists per century are sufficient to silence most performers or artists to maintain the "company" line.

Stanley Dyrector has transcribed a number of interviews he's done with the victims (martyrs) of the signal blacklist of the twentieth century, which did the job in blanketing dissent in this country into the twenty-first century. He's done his job in salvaging humanity. It's up to us to see his work is not wasted or pointless.

Senator Joseph McCarthy

Introduction

Stop the presses! – Breaking News! – There is a NEW HOLLYWOOD BLACKLIST: Yes, it is ironic that in today's jargon, the blacklist means something totally different. Every generation changes the meanings of words. Bad used to mean bad. Now it means good. "That's really bad, man."

Today the Hollywood Blacklist is known for the best unproduced screenplays. I kid you not; this actually exists now, in Tinseltown, USA. Almost every writer I meet nowadays would love to get on that list. I must say, a couple of old timers I spoke to about it were struck with ire and disbelief when I mentioned it.

Many scripts on the new blacklist have, and will, be made into movies. My, how times have changed! Nobody wanted to be on the Blacklist of the late '40s and 1950s, because it meant you were unemployable. You lost your means to make a living and you either left the country and worked abroad or you changed professions. Families suffered, as you will discover in this book, and suffice to say, some very talented, sensitive people couldn't take it and had breakdowns and committed suicide.

I was fortunate enough to meet a lot of blacklisted writers after the fact. I am sorry I was not able to get Helen and Alfred Levitt, but Alfred had become devastatingly ill, which I learned when I sought him out. Helen had passed away earlier.

When I was compiling this book from the many interviews I did, I noticed that in quite a few of them (the 'one-on-ones' that I did with my 4 guests on the library shows), they tended to repeat themselves. They probably didn't remember that they had told that same story on a past show because they had probably told those stories thousands of times over the years. And I didn't remember whether they had told me that story in our conversations off the air. Anyway, I edited out some, but not all, because I feel that any good story is worth repeating.

One of my motives for why I wanted to work on this book and complete it was because of friends who had been blacklisted. We all didn't start out to be friends, it just happened for me along the way of pursuing and getting to know these individuals who were persecuted by the madmen inquisitors of the day, with the help of the United States Government, so sadly, I say.

HUAC was the acronym for the House Un-American Activities Committee (1947-1975), which historians dubbed the McCarthy Era – the era of witch-hunts. I'd like you to know that during World War II, there were many servicemen, Party members, and 'fellow travelers' who served honorably and with valor in combat and in important jobs who, when they resumed their careers in entertainment, suddenly found themselves blacklisted for past alliances. How cruel for that to happen to those who distinguished themselves with such valor in combat. Also, let us not forget the home front, where many loyal Americans who would later on become blacklistees helped their country with good deeds during the war effort as volunteers for the USO, entertaining troops, and so on. They were mostly unsung for their dedication in doing their share to keep America free. When you read on in these interviews, I'm sure you will find that out for yourself. But suffice to say, all my guests were wounded in some way or another during the era of the Blacklist. Brrrr! I shiver because of what those committees did to American citizens. They intimidated witnesses by making them grovel and pitting them against each other. But think of it, Dear Reader; at one time the Communist Party was on the ballot. Yes, you could have voted them in or out just like the Democrats and Republicans. So even though back in the day it may not have been politically correct to help support black civil rights, women's equal rights, labor rights, and a host of other issues, my guests did. They were sympathetic to causes. They paid the price. I learned that in the early days, many met in secret, in small groups. Today, similar groups would be out in the open, and you'd call them activists, or citizens for change, or some such thing.

This Blacklist thing happened when I was a little kid growing up in Brooklyn, New York, and who knew from politics? I was not political. I'd heard or read stories that colored people were being lynched in the South, and that always gave me a lousy feeling in my stomach. How helpless I felt!

I'll tell you how I met a few of my octogenarian and nonagenarian blacklisted friends, who were guests on my shows. We all belonged to the same Guilds: SAG/AFTRA, or the Writers Guild of America (West). I am in all of those unions.

But first, before we go further in this book, you will hear references made to Waldo Salt. My wife Joyce and I met Waldo Salt in the late '70s when we attended a WGAw Writers' Conference up in the UCLA Conference Center in Lake Arrowhead. He was there with his wife, Eve Merriam, the poet/writer. He was an affable and gentle man. Both he and Eve were generous. He was heralded with many Writers Guild Awards, including two Oscars. Several years later, we'd see him here and there, but I'll never forget the day he was eating an ice cream cone outside, in the back of the drugstore entrance by the parking lot on Fairfax and Sunset in Hollywood. When he saw us it was like Joyce and I were his old friends, and so we talked for quite some time. He never had an attitude of big shot, or of being better than you. He was beautiful.

My first interview with a blacklisted writer came in 1994 when Richard Powell (known as "The Other Dick Powell") appeared on my cable-TV show, then known as Senior Prom. My interview with Powell sparked a renewal of my interest in the Blacklist Era and I began to seek out other writers and actors who had lived through it.

I met some writers through my wife, Joyce, who was then a member of the Writers Guild Women's Committee. One of the writers I met through her involvement was Norma Barzman. How wonderful it was – and still is – to have a pal like Norma. It was she who recently introduced me to Marsha Hunt.

Some of my memories about how I got to meet some of my TV show guests are vivid. I had difficulty trying to get to actor/teacher Jeff Corey because I didn't know him and because he lived in Malibu, where he'd taught in the Blacklist days in his garage (his students included the likes of Jack Nicholson, James Dean, Jane Fonda, Barbra Streisand, and Robin Williams). A fellow WGA member gave me Jeff's number. I called and we set up a date to meet in a Hollywood TV studio. The occasion is etched in my mind. He and his wife, Hope, came in all the way from Malibu. He was no youngster, but he was as sharp as a tack. Before we started the show and the TV cameras were about to roll, he told me we should be silent for a few moments until I got the signal to begin my introduction. I cheated and saw Jeff close his eyes and I believed he was with his muse there. Here I was with a man who, after his passing not many months later, was honored at the Dorothy Chandler Pavilion in Los Angeles for being a giant of theatre. His portrayal of Polonius in Shakespeare's Hamlet was brilliant. On that occasion, Gordon Davidson of the Music Center and many other stars paid Jeff Corey homage.

I met Abraham Polonsky, blacklisted screen and television writer, sometime in 1999. I had learned that he was living in Beverly Hills and I thought that he would be the perfect guest for my television show. Through the Writers Guild of America West, of which we were both members, I was able to arrange to call him and invite him to be a guest on my show. We agreed to meet at his Beverly Hills condo about a week later. Abe was a lean, spry, spirited, and feisty man in his late eighties. As we went to his large living room, I glanced at a small Rouault painting on the wall. Abe sat in a favorite chair overlooking a courtyard as we spoke. I explained my interview would be about how his long career began and how the Blacklist affected his life. Abe's response was not what

I'd expected. It went something like this: "Why should I do a show with you? I've done lots of shows. I've talked about my career and been interviewed in books, et cetera." Abe's barrage of reasons for not doing my show was initially overwhelming, until I sensed that I shouldn't treat him with the great deference I actually felt but rather should just respond in kind. "I know I'm not Charley Rose or any of the other big shots on television, but my show is seen by people, and lots of people are interested in the Hollywood Blacklist and what happened to people, how they got hurt by it, writers such as yourself." Abe responded with a dry smile and said, "You know, you talk like me." He meant, of course, my New York accent. I'm from Brooklyn and he was from the lower East Side. And suddenly we were just two former New York kids having a conversation about how frustrating the movie business was. I was thrilled that he was going to do the show, but the frustrations were not yet over. We agreed to an open date a couple of weeks later, but when I called him a couple of days before show time to remind him, he was sick and said he wouldn't be able to make it. I had to cancel my precious TV time because I didn't have a plan-B guest available. Finally Abe did our first half-hour show and, as my director was a very pretty young lady, Mr. Polonsky appeared to be extremely pleased. On that show, I learned that his full name was Abraham Lincoln Polonsky—a name he professed not to appreciate (although his father had promised that he someday would). We did a second show about a week later. We had planned to do a third show but he died before it could be arranged. We used to go to Canter's Delicatessen with my wife, Joyce, and I miss his dry wit and the corned beef on rye with pickle, on a Friday night. It was our great loss and a reminder that we should gather oral histories while we can.

I met Robert Lees through a mutual friend in the Writers Guild of America/West sometime in 2000 or thereabouts. He was a most engaging man; there was always a merry twinkle in his eyes, and he was a man of good cheer and compassion. He did two interviews with me: one was with a group of four blacklisted Hollywood screenwriters, and then this one. Bob, it is most important to say, was a forgiving man to his accusers, one in particular whom he mentions. Robert was a very trusting person who'd never lock his front door. To do that in a world of sharks and other evils was not wise and it led to his unfortunate demise. He was over 90 years old, in good health and amazingly vibrant. He did things like a man half his age. My wife Joyce and I delighted in his friendship and company. We will miss him very much.

I met John Randolph at Hindi Brooks' house at a July 4th party. I approached him and his face lit up so brightly, it could melt an iceberg and that's how I obtained his interview.

By the way, my first Hollywood Blacklist Show at the Frances Howard Goldwyn Library in Hollywood was disrupted by an intimidating, misinformed audience member as you'll discover in Chapter 1.

Chapter One

THE STANLEY DYRECTOR SHOW

"THE HOLLYWOOD BLACKLIST, PART 1"

06/12/01

Producer/Host
STANLEY DYRECTOR

With Special Guests
JEAN ROUVEROL, BERNARD GORDON
OLIVER CRAWFORD, ROBERT LEES

STAN

Hello, and welcome to *The Stanley Dyrector Show*. We are privileged to broadcast Show Number One of our three part series on the Hollywood Blacklist from the Frances Howard Goldwyn Library in Hollywood, California—an ironic location. Let me give you a brief rundown on the House Un-American Activities Committee (or HUAC), which frightened Hollywood studio bosses and caused the Blacklist. Its first victims of hate and intimidation were the Hollywood Ten, who were subpoenaed in 1947 to Washington, DC to testify about their membership in the Communist Party. They pleaded the First Amendment.

A few years later, our distinguished guests were named and blacklisted as Communists.

Jean Rouverol started her career as an actress at MGM. She's written screenplays, fiction and non-fiction. Jean was married to the blacklisted screen writer, Hugo Butler. Her book is called *Refugees from Hollywood*.

1

Guests & Host show Audience

The Hollywood Ten in 1948 with their attorneys:
From left—front row: Herbert Biberman, attorneys Martin
Popper and Robert W. Kenny, Albert Maltz, Lester Cole,
--second row: Dalton Trumbo, John Howard Lawson, Alvah
Bessie, Samuel Ornitz —*back row:* Ring Lardner Jr., Edward
Dmytryk, Adrian Scott).

2

Bernard Gordon was a story editor at Paramount. He's a screen writer-producer who wrote such films as *55 Days at Peking*, the original *The Thin Red Line*, and his book is *Hollywood Exile*.

Oliver Crawford was an actor on Broadway who became a playwright, screen, and television writer. He wrote *Quincy* and *Starsky and Hutch*. Oliver's play is called *Ollie, Folly and the Blacklist*.

Robert Lees was a dancer and actor at MGM. Working as screenwriters, Lees and his collaborator, Fred Rinaldo, wrote Robert Benchley shorts and Abbott & Costello movies.

On Show Number One, our guests will describe their lives before the Blacklist. On Show Number Two, they will talk about how they got blacklisted and the effect of the Blacklist. Show Number Three will be about their lives after the Blacklist.

Jean, can you take us back to another time and tell us how and why you got involved with the Communist Party?

JEAN

Gladly. And I hope that you'll excuse me for using cue cards. I'm turning eighty-five next month and, doggone it, my memory isn't worth a darn. So, I need help. Anyway, the day that Waldo Salt, who was then a junior writer at Metro, introduced me to his office mate, Hugo Butler, it was, I think, sometime in November 1936. I'd just gotten back to Hollywood from my second Broadway flop. One lasted three weeks, one lasted two. So much for theatre. And I, at barely seventeen, had been 'discovered' in a play at the Pasadena Playhouse and signed to a Hollywood contract, which I didn't really want. I took theatre seriously but I thought movies were just a loused up version of plays. While I was at Paramount, and immediately after, I had played W.C. Field's daughter in *It's A Gift*—if you ever watch old movies—a schizophrenic in Walter Wanger's *Private Worlds*, leads in a few westerns and a Republic mystery and cameos or character parts in bigger pictures.

That day, it took me about thirty seconds to fall wildly in love with Hugo and within five months, we were married and moved into a little apartment on North Beachwood, about five blocks from here. Hugo who—unlike me—really understood and loved movies, was quickly writing, or co-writing, his way out of the junior writer department with pictures like *Christmas Carol, Huckleberry Finn, Lassie Come Home,* and the two Edison pictures—while I was heading out at dawn for sometimes leads, sometimes cameos in *Stage Door, The Road Back,* a couple of *Crime Doesn't Pay* shorts (co-written by my friend, Bobby Lees, here). And when successive pregnancies began to make movie work impossible, I started a third-year run on a much loved radio series called *One Man's Family.* Does anybody remember, anybody here old enough to remember that one? It was during this period that I also got a junior writer contract at Metro and began that career too. Hugo had already become active in the early struggles at the Writer's Guild, Screen Writer's Guild, and we had made friends, significantly, with a couple of new recruits to Hollywood named Ring Lardner, Jr. and Dalton Trumbo. By now, the political atmosphere of Hollywood was changing. My fellow panelists will tell you all about that.

We were all equally affected by the rise of fascism abroad and the grim face of the Great Depression at home. And Hugo, in the meantime, had been hired to adapt two of his favorite books: the Depression love story *All Brides Are Beautiful,* which became the movie *From This Day Forward,* and later, *Hold Autumn In Your Hand,* a haunting book about a family of sharecroppers, directed by Jean Renoir and released as *The Southerner.* Altogether, when Waldo Salt invited us to join the Communist Party, we didn't need any convincing at all. When Hugo was drafted late in World War II, he went off to training camp convinced that he was joining a "People's Army' to fight a 'People's War." Think how long that lasted—just about the time it took for him to get through basic training. Boy, was he anxious to come home. When the birth of our third child made him eligible for release, he was only too happy. In his absence, however, I had begun selling novellas to *McCalls.* The first one—now remember he's getting $35 a month as a buck private—I sold for five thousand. And, oh boy, did it sound good. Anyway, having been placed on leave from the Party during his Army service—as I was—Hugo decided once home to rejoin. But about my rejoining, he said, "Listen, with three kids, the radio job, the PTA and your writing, Christ, I'd never see you." So I didn't rejoin but I remained a staunch Marxist.

Once again, we plunged into our busy lives. We mortgaged our souls to buy a big old turn-of-the-century craftsman house up on Briarcliff, just off Canyon Drive. You know that area? And then in 1947, with the Cold War in full cry, Trumbo and Lardner and eight other of the Hollywood Ten were called before HUAC–and I'll tell you later how that affected us.

STAN
Bernard Gordon, can you tell us your story, please?

BERNARD
Well, I was born in New Britain, Connecticut, but I really grew up in the Bronx, so I have to confess and you can probably hear the accent is still there. I'm a Bronx boy. And I grew up through the Depression and I knew lines of people waiting outside in the cold for a cup of coffee or a little soup. I knew the fact that peoples'— everything was wrong in this country. It looked like capitalism just wasn't working at all. That peoples' furniture was being thrown out on the street; there were no jobs; there was something like forty percent unemployment. My father had a little hardware store and he lost everything because of the crash. I went to City College and I decided I wanted to be a movie maker. And so, with a $16 share-the-ride to California, to Los Angeles, I finally got here with $10 in my pocket and here I am. I got a job as a reader at Paramount, and soon it was understood that I had a radical bent and I was recruited into the Party, which was very easy for me to do because I had lived through the Depression; I had seen the things that were wrong in this country. I knew about racism. I knew about unemployment. I knew about the Depression. It seemed to an awful lot of us in those days that capitalism really was a failed system and that the future belonged to socialism of one kind or another. So I joined.

In 1947, when the first hearings were held in Washington, that's when the Hollywood Ten appeared, I was named by someone I didn't know as a communist sympathizer. Some attorney who knew me here because of my trade union activity, got up and said, "You can't do this. Mr. Gordon is not here; he can't defend himself," but of course he was gaveled down. I found out about it in the trade

M.J. Parnell Thomas (HUC)

Martin Dies (HUC)

Jean Rouverol

Bernard Gordon

Oliver Crawford

Robert Lees

papers the next day. At this time I was an assistant story editor, and nothing was said at the Studio—this was Paramount—until a couple months later. And at the end of December when my wife and I were expecting our first child, I got a Christmas present of having been fired after seven years. I consider myself prematurely blacklisted. I'm the first person I know who was actually fired for political reasons in this town.

STAN

On our next show, we're going to cover the full Blacklist. Oliver Crawford, can you please tell us what it was like before you were blacklisted?

OLIVER

Well, I was born and raised in Chicago during a tough period when there was an attempted Capone takeover of the dairy industry. My father was a milkman and he was one of the organizers of the American Federation of Labor in that city. As a fourteen-year-old boy, I would help him out. We had these big wagons with these Clydesdale horses you see pulling beer. And he carried a gun and I was terrified. Now in those days, you've got to understand, there were no unions, no minimum wage, no pensions, no Social Security, no Medicare–none of the things that we know about–it was strictly a laissez-faire system. I can recall working in a department store from nine in the morning until nine at night for $1.75. Or I'd go to an unemployment line, where they would hire over a weekend, same department store. There'd be a line; I'd take my place, and I'd sell my place for a quarter to some married man who had a family. At any rate, it was very easy to be radicalized. Certainly I was receptive to the social ferment. I was only a kid and in those days the Communist Party was a legal entity, even in its most vilified period. It was never outlawed. At any rate, I was proselytized. However I did not join until after I came to Hollywood after World War II. But during those formative years in Chicago, I did hang around people who lived in a world of paper, books, and ideas. And also, there was a great rumor that the Communist Party espoused free love. Well, I had juices and they were certainly most attractive. Let me tell you, that's a base canard.

Maybe these other guys were luckier—not me. At any rate, that was my Chicago phase.

I got married in '41 and was drafted in 1943. Three and a half years in the Army overseas, came back, and we had no children. And, of course, the two centers of entertainment were largely West Coast, Hollywood, and East Coast, New York. So I was in the Pacific Theater. My wife met me. And I was then mostly a young actor. I'd done some special service work in the Army jeep teams. We went into places that the USOs wouldn't go to, that were inaccessible. We were two jeep teams. Mickey Rooney was on one of them. Anyway, I came back. I got a fairly honorable discharge. And my wife was very practical. She was a legal secretary and volunteered her services to a then-premier acting organization called The Actors Lab and she arranged for me to have an audition. It was very difficult, because they were an offshoot, some of you may recall, it goes way back, of the old Group Theatre in New York. And I did a scene from *Watch on the Rhine* and my three judges were Anthony Quinn and Danny Mann, who was a fine director, and the head of the Lab, and I passed it and I became an actor, scrambling for parts. I wasn't tall and I wasn't good looking and so on, so it was pretty rough. In the meantime, I always liked to write. I was always doodling. Also, at that time, something called television was coming along and screenwriters disdained it. It was below them and they felt it was, you know, just a box.

STAN

Very good, Ollie. I'm going to get to that part a little later. Now I'm going to get to Mr. Robert Lees. Robert can you tell us, please, what you did before you were blacklisted?

ROBERT

Well, after all, I'm in kind of a strange position, because I was born in San Francisco, in kind of a middle-class Jewish family. I didn't have any of the problems that some of you guys had and I was a star, kind of, as an actor at Lowell High School and I was deciding I was going to be an actor. I came down to Los Angeles at the time of the Depression in 1930, to go to UCLA because

8

my father's business at this point fell apart. It was the start of the Depression, but he fell apart a little earlier. So when I came to Los Angeles and I was at UCLA, my father said, "What are you doing there? We can't afford to do this."

Well, I had a connection through my father with Metro-Goldwyn-Mayer, so I went there to become an actor, as a chorus boy. I danced in *Dancing Lady*. I was a bellboy in *Grand Hotel*, I was in *Rasputin and the Empress*, and I was with Greta Garbo in a thing called *As You Desire Me*, with Melvyn Douglas. I was the boatman; they curled up my hair. I had long black hair which they curled up. And then I tried to dance in *Dancing Lady*. And I didn't know how to do a time step, couldn't learn it; stuffed my shoe with toilet paper so I would look taller. The shoe came off while I was dancing. The toilet paper came out, serpentine. They stopped everything and said, "What the hell is going on?" And I was very embarrassed but the dance director said, "I've never seen anything quite like this." He says, "You're too short" (I was taller than he was) "to be in the chorus. You can't dance, but you've got a lot of guts. I tell you what; I'll make you an assistant." So that was the start of my career. And when I found out that I could have a screen test, I wrote it. Unfortunately I wrote it, or fortunately, I wrote it but unfortunately I was a lousy actor. So they turned around and said, "The acting is lousy, the writing is good. You should be a junior writer." So I became a junior writer at Metro-Goldwyn-Mayer at the same time that the Screen Writers Guild was starting to be organized and all the things that Bernie Gordon was talking about.

Hollywood was really my kindergarten for being progressive. My collaborator came from Dartmouth, where he had learned a lot, where he had met Buddy Schulberg and Maurice Rapf, who had gone to the Soviet Union and come back saying, "It's a wonderful place." And all the kids and all the guys in my generation—we're all pretty much the same generation—and Hugo. We're all taken into this wonderful spirit of 'we can do something about it.' In Hollywood, it was rampant. We had the Anti-Nazi League; we had the Anti-Fascist League against fascism. We were doing ambulances for Spain. Everything at this particular moment said, if you're a writer and you're a progressive, and you're organizing the Screen Writers Guild—I'm an absolute charter member— you'd better do it with an organization that knows what it's doing, because all these things were related. And the Communist Party at that time knew they were related and was functioning in all those areas, and I functioned with them. And I learned a great deal. So from my San Francisco Republican background, I became pretty much politicized. But in the meantime, Fred Rinaldo and I went into the Shorts Department as part of a group that we called 'The Brain Trust'—Alvin Josephy, Fred Rinaldo, myself and a girl called Nikki Jeston. Nikki was very, very great at a party when she was drunk and was very witty, but couldn't write a line of that funny stuff on paper. But they put us all together and we were writing together, and when that fell apart, Fred and I became a team in the Shorts Department at Metro-Goldwyn-Mayer, where we did Robert Benchleys and Pete Smiths and *Crime Doesn't Pay*, which Jean was in. And we did a lot of stuff like that. And then finally we came up from that area into doing a lot of good comedies—*Abbott & Costello Meet Frankenstein* and seven others, and Olsen and Johnson and Martin and Lewis. And we had a wonderful career doing all these things as the war came along and then came the period of the Cold War and then came the period of the Blacklist and the Hollywood Ten. And that's when the shit hit the fan, so to speak.

STAN
But before that happened, didn't you write a movie for Desi Arnaz that did well?

ROBERT
Among other things, we did a thing called *Night in Havana*, which Desi Arnaz, with his drums and so forth, was in. It was about a contest in Cuba for the best band, and our producer at that time said, "There's this crazy character we don't know what to do with. Why don't you see what you can help him do?" And we came back with, "This guy's pretty damn smart," which he was. And I think Fred and I should have had a chance to do I Love Lucy. But we never had an opportunity to say, "Desi, remember us? Comedy

team? How about Lucy?" We were dead. We had already tried to do a Benchley short for television. I destroyed my house.

Incidentally, I had a wonderful background and career, because I had three in-help. They were Japanese. My wife was working with the Party at the moment and they were trying to get the Japanese, who were coming out of the concentration camps, jobs. And she went to all our friends and said, "do something," because these people didn't know where to go. So we happened to be lucky enough to have a mother and three daughters who stayed with us. She put them through school, through college. I don't know where she got the money. I had paid her some money but I was broke; but she was a wonderful mother and she knew how to save money. So we had three in-help, a Buick convertible, lots of credit, money in the bank, and it was supposed that I was going to overthrow the government by force and violence. I think this is pretty ridiculous.

STAN

That is pretty ridiculous. You know, I want to note that we have a gentleman in the audience who was also blacklisted and he's in a book called *Tender Comrades*, a very dear gentleman by the name of Julian Zimet. And now I would like to ask our audience if anybody has a question for our group on what they've heard so far. Yes, Sir?

MAN IN AUDIENCE

Yes, my question is to anybody who wishes to answer it. Going through the prospectus and listening to what you said, I'm wondering where is, as part of your panel discussion, in terms of equality, the other side of the picture? We're talking about Anti-Fascism, Anti-Nazism, what about Anti-Communism, one of the greatest evils besides Nazism?

STAN

Okay, this gentleman poses a very good question. Oliver, you wanted to answer that?

ROBERT

We'll all have a crack at that.

OLIVER

Don't confuse the later climate with what existed then: the social ferment. It was not the Cold War; that was invented after the war by Winston Churchill, who spoke of the Iron Curtain, and much later by Ronald Reagan, with the Evil Empire. You've got to understand, communism was in the forefront of virtually every social advantage that we have today. And I'm talking minimum wage; I'm talking the Wagner Act.

MAN IN THE AUDIENCE

What planet are you on? Communism killed more people than the Nazis ever had a chance to kill. Stalin was a mass murderer.

STAN

Sir, wait a minute, hold on.

OLIVER

You asked a question.

MAN IN THE AUDIENCE

You're saying what wonderful people these communists were. They were bad.

STAN

Oliver, this gentleman asks a good question. We have discovered that Stalin was a son-of-a-gun.

OLIVER

We had nothing to do with Stalin.

STAN

I would like Robert Lees to address this gentleman.

ROBERT

I think we have a man here who's really taking the other side vociferously without looking at what the situation was really. The Roosevelt New Deal was considered communist, because he did all these things that supposedly made him a traitor to his class. We were all people who remembered Roosevelt as saving the United States and capitalism. We were really with that same attitude of that time. As Ollie said, this was a very legal situation. There was a Socialist Party, there was a Communist Party. It was there for a long time. There was nothing illegal about it. We are not Russians. We are not spies. We are American citizens and considered ourselves to be very loyal Americans. What came after, to turn us into being villains, has now been changed a little bit. You're a little behind the times. Because we did not inform—which we'll get into. We did not do these things.

We felt that this country needed what was Roosevelt's program and we were fostering it. There was nothing illegal; there was nothing dangerous. If we were to do bombing like there was done here, we would have been electrocuted. If we had done anything at all that was illegal, we would have been taken by the police or by whomever it would be. We didn't. We opened our mouths. That's all we did. And that was illegal during the McCarthy period.

STAN

Bernard Gordon, go ahead.

BERNARD

I'd like to remind the gentleman that, of course, he's entitled to his opinion, as I hope I'm entitled to mine. But when I joined the Communist Party in 1942, there was a war on. The Nazis were destroying, had already destroyed, most of Europe or captured it. Roosevelt and America were sending planes and tanks and food and everything possible to the Russians, to try to stop the Nazis. And, in fact, it was the Russians—under Stalin—who, I hope you realize, did stop the Nazis.

MAN IN THE AUDIENCE
They supported the Nazis up to 1941.

BERNARD
I think you ought to get him up here to be one of the speakers.

STAN
Sir, let Mr. Gordon answer the question.

WOMAN'S VOICE
Calm down, sir, calm down.

MAN'S VOICE
You will not be allowed to disrupt this meeting, sir.

STAN
Hold on, sir, for one minute. Bernard, please continue.

BERNARD
I simply wanted to point out that at the time most of us were joining the Party, or in the Party, we were together with the majority of Americans in supporting the Russians in the war against Hitler. And, in fact, it was the Russians who did defeat Hitler more than anyone else, if you remember. Our position in the Party was that capitalism, as I told you before, was in terrible shape. We were people who were for unemployment insurance, for helping people get jobs. We were against racism. These are things we were for. We were not for Stalin as such, although at that time a great American writer went to the Soviet Union and said, "I have seen the future, and it works." Well, that was wrong. It didn't work. We were wrong about some of these things.

STAN
We are wrapping it up, folks. We will continue our conversation on our next program on the Blacklist and I want you guys to tune in to our next show about the Hollywood Blacklist, when we'll talk in more detail about what happened when these

folks were blacklisted. Let me say goodnight, Godspeed, and God love you. Jean, I want to thank you; Bernard, I want to thank you; Oliver, I want to thank you; Robert Lees, you made me laugh a lot with *Abbott & Costello Meet Frankenstein*. So thank you very much.

THE STANLEY DYRECTOR SHOW

"THE HOLLYWOOD BLACKLIST, PART 2"

Producer/Host
STANLEY DYRECTOR

With Special Guests
JEAN ROUVEROL, BERNARD GORDON
OLIVER CRAWFORD, ROBERT LEES

STAN

Hello, ladies and gentlemen. Welcome to *The Stanley Dyrector Show* again. We are privileged to broadcast Part 2 of our three-part series on the Hollywood Blacklist from the Frances Howard Goldwyn Library in Hollywood, California.

Jean, take us back to the events in your life when you and your husband, Hugo Butler, were blacklisted.

JEAN

Well, by late January of '51—forgive my cue cards again, better than trusting my ad libs—here's how things stood. Our friends were still in various, quote, "houses of correction," and how's that for a euphemism; the federal pens. A Hollywood graylist was still in force, which we'd managed to survive by Hugo's co-writing *A Woman of Distinction*. He'd done a few other scripts too and I'd co-written an original for Paul Henry, sold three more novellas to *McCall's*. We'd had a fourth child, nervously rented out our big, expensive house and, and leased a smaller, cheaper one. Before too long, we'd sell the big one. And now we were working on a little domestic comedy for Harold Hecht and Burt Lancaster.

17

When Hugo learned that HUAC had begun a new sweep, and that Waldo Salt had just received a subpoena, he decided that he'd better not come home that day after work, just in case. "I tried the army, he said, and I know I wouldn't like jail."

So I was having dinner alone with the children that night when the doorbell rang. They wanted Hugo, of course. Terrified, I got rid of them, and from then on it was just pure panic. Phoning Hugo at a restaurant to warn him, dividing the kids up between their two grandmothers, finding friends with spare beds to put us up, and going to work at Columbia every morning in the clothes we'd slept in, which were badly rumpled by then, and terrified that we'd find a U.S. Marshall waiting for us in the front office to give us a subpoena. Thank heaven they were too busy looking for other people. Since Hugo's name hadn't been released, we were able to finish the Hecht-Lancaster assignment and Hugo switched over to co-writing something called *The Big Night* with his friend, director Joe Losey, who was also on the run by then. When Trumbo got home from jail, with two months off for good behavior, we made our way to his ranch to make plans.

Trumbo had read that there was a very good American school in Mexico City and since he and Cleo had three children to our four, we determined that as soon as they had sold the ranch and had some money, we'd all set out. We had to live pretty make-shift lives until almost November. In early November, we rendezvoused with the Trumbos in San Diego and took off with two cars, a jeep with a tear-drop trailer, four adults, seven children, the Trumbo sheep dog and the Butler Siamese cat, and a wandering strep throat which felled a different child at every stop. It took us quite a while to get down. Once settled in Mexico City, life often proved worrisome but always exciting. Hugo's first job down there was to revise, under a pseudonym of course, his own screenplay of *Robinson Crusoe* with Spanish refugee director Luis Bunuel. That's the one with Dan O'Herlihy. Hugo found Bunuel to be quirky, brilliant, and wonderful. Later, he'd do two more scripts with him, one not made but which sold to MGM, and another, *The Young One*, which would get an award at the Cannes Film Festival. He also made two docudramas: one on bullfighting which won an Oscar nomination and a Flaherty award under a *nom de plume*, and one later about the first little league team that Mexico was ever allowed to send up to the world championships and which won, with a no-hitter. The smallest, poorest kids in the history of the league. You can imagine how Mexico took that one. It was released in both languages and filmed down there and shown up here on television, called *How Tall Is the Giant*. Hugo's apolitical but stubbornly loyal director friend, Bob Aldrich, was also a source of support. One little adventure picture for Hugo, and for both of us, an adaptation of one of my *McCall's* novellas, which made it to the screen as *Autumn Leaves*, with Joan Crawford. I also fell heir to an unlikely assignment with Hugo's very Republican father, revising the story of Max Reinhardt's epic *The Miracle*, of all things. Our job was to get it off the Catholic Index and then do a screenplay, and we succeeded. The Catholics were delighted. And late in the decade, glory be to heaven, I sold two more novellas to the slicks, under my own name. That was about 1958. Imagine how we felt about that. Altogether, our lives in Mexico were astonishingly rich.

We found a house in San Angel, which we had come to love more than any we'd ever had, next door to Diego Rivera's studio. We made profound new friendships with families on the run from various parts of the States. There were the deaths of parents, the births of two more babies, the loss of beloved animals, and small children became adolescents. We had to live totally non-political lives, in spite of which we were constantly under scrutiny by the FBI, as I learned later when I sent for our FBI files under the Freedom of Information Act. I have those, by the way, with me. And there was the bitter discovery, in 1956, of guess what, the Stalin atrocities. My book goes into how we tried desperately to deal with that one. It was a very tough time for all of us. And finally, there was the cumulative effect of all this on Hugo. The ever-so-subtle personality changes, evidence (though I chose to ignore it) of the stored up tensions which would really change our lives in ways I couldn't, in those years, even guess at.

STAN

Thank you. Bernard, can you tell us how the blacklist affected you?

19

BERNARD

Well, I'd like to say that after having been fired in 1947 by Paramount, I had to make a living somehow or other. So with my old friend from college days, from high school days, we decided to become writers. And we got some jobs on some low budget pictures. The first one was called *The Millen Case* at Columbia. To give you an idea of what the atmosphere was like in this country at the time, the Party wanted us to include, as much as possible, black people, or other minority people, as characters in the story. So we put in a black taxi driver. When the producer read it, he crossed it out. We said, "Why are you crossing it out?" He said, "Why is it in here?" We said, "Because it's right, it's real, it felt true." He said, "It would only make trouble for us in the South." At the same time, the woman who became my wife was the Executive Secretary at the Hollywood Canteen. And the big thing about that canteen was that they tried to have total democracy. Any serviceman was allowed to come in, to eat, to listen to the music, to dance. But the Hollywood studios were worried about what would happen if a black soldier or sailor should dance with a white actress, a white woman. Well, my wife finally got them to agree, in spite of the fears of the Hollywood producers, that any hostess could refuse to dance with anybody who asked her, whether he was too tall or too short or too sweaty or too hairy, without making any reference to color. That seemed to work except that the Shore Patrolman, who was there to keep order for the Navy, could not stand seeing a black soldier or sailor dance with a white woman and he would drag them into the mens room and beat them up. When my wife found out about this, she and Bette Davis went down to the Captain of the Navy, downtown, to ask him to do something about this and get rid of Mickey. That was his name. I'll never forget Mickey. Of course, the Captain was very, very impressed to see Bette Davis there. On the other hand, he was a southerner and he probably did not feel that what Mickey was doing was so bad. But, when my wife and Bette Davis suggested that Mickey be sent out into the Pacific to fight the Japanese, instead of fighting our people here at the Canteen, Bette Davis or no, this was too much for the Captain. He said that he would just take care of it. He'd see that Mickey acted correctly from there on. Well, nothing changed, except that the people at the Canteen, under my wife's direction—she was not my wife yet—went into the mens room as often as possible to try to keep Mickey from behaving this way. At the same time, all of the bands, who were always there at the Canteen, did not mix. Probably people today can't realize that the Musicians Union had two locals, a white one and a black one and they did not mix. This was what America was like at that time.

Now for my personal experiences. The conditions were so bad here that we decided to go to Mexico. We preceded the Butlers, but I soon ran out of money and I couldn't get any work there, so we came back. Then my friends said there was a possibility of getting work in Europe. I went to Europe. I didn't get any work there and I came back. By this time, my wife was ready to sell our ten-year-old Chevy in order to buy food, but by some miracle, I got to work at Universal writing pictures and I had great success there. I wrote the first starring picture for Tony Curtis, called *Flesh and Fury*. I wrote the first real starring picture for Rock Hudson, *The Lawless Breed*, and they were talking about a contract for me. This was 1952 and I had not been blacklisted yet. But then I found out that there was subpoena out for me and instead of getting a contract, I was fired. And there was a man sitting outside the door of our house, a little place on Curson Avenue, here. And I didn't want to take the subpoena because we all felt that if we didn't make an appearance before the Committee, we wouldn't be publicly named as "Reds" and we would fall through the cracks and maybe we could continue working.

STAN

Bernard, I'm going to talk to Oliver Crawford now, but I want to hear more about that on our next show. Oliver, what was your experience on the blacklist?

OLIVER

I would like to preface that, because it's so difficult to envision the climate. To explain the Depression is like explaining the Crusades. You have to realize that even before the HUAC activities in 1947, that back in 1938, Shirley Temple was named as a communist dupe. It's a matter of record. Frank Sinatra was named twelve times. I mean, the political change was seismic. The Republicans were getting back at Roosevelt. Remember, he was elected four times and they could never forgive him for that. Anyway, that was the political climate.

All right. I got back. And I had my audition. As I said earlier, screenwriters were not doing television. I wasn't getting much work as an actor, just appeared in a few pictures in meaningless, small parts. So I started writing. I got $100 for something called *Fireside Theatre*; fifteen-minute dramas. Some friends of mine were getting into it, and they got into it very cheaply. I got my $100. It was picked up by CBS. And I was promptly sued for plagiarism. They named J. Walter Thompson, CBS and Frank Wisbar Productions, and lastly, me. I had no deep pockets; the others did. Well, I was very embarrassed, and many years later, the original writer thanked me for stealing his work. I wasn't aware that I was doing it, but I had been influenced by a radio show I had heard many years earlier and my subconscious came back. The writer told me he got more money in settlement than the aggregate of all the re-broadcasts and said, "You're welcome to steal anything I've got."

STAN

Ollie, thank you. I have to go on now, with Robert Lees. We'll come back to you later. Bob, go ahead, give us your take on your blacklist.

ROBERT

I'm going to try and go fast on this cause I never know where it starts here. But actually, I'm one of the few people that went to Washington right after the Hollywood Ten. I was on the stand for an hour and a half, right after Sterling Hayden named me. He said he couldn't remember anybody's name, but he remembered mine and he remembered Abe Polonsky, so we were then coming up next after this. And I was on the stand for an hour and a half. I left to go home knowing I was blacklisted and I didn't know what to do. I had no more jobs, because if you did not cooperate with the House Un-American Activities Committee, you were automatically blacklisted by the studios. The Ten were fined by the Committee and sent to jail. We took the Fifth Amendment and the First. And because we couldn't testify against ourselves, the Committee was helpless. But the producers said, "If you don't cooperate with the committee, you will not be hired." So the second session of the Fifth Amendment group, which I was part of, we were the blacklisted group, because we could not work. That was the punishment. The Committee didn't punish us; the industry did. We couldn't work.

I went to Tucson, Arizona with my brother-in-law, who was going to open a restaurant in a hotel. He had the lease on it. I became the Maitre d'. I didn't know what to do with the Caesar Salads, and they wound up on the floor. I called them Sid Caesar Salads. I had no idea what I was doing as the Maitre d'. The girls, thank god, they said to me, "What can we do, we like you. What do we do?" I said to them, "Whatever you do, do it. Fill the sugar bowls." They filled the sugar bowls, the salt shakers, they set the things up, they made the schedule, and made me look good. But then, I was in Tucson for a year and a half, and my brother-in-law left. The hotel kept me on, which I'll tell you about later, because the FBI was chasing me all over the place after I left Hollywood. They came to Tucson. When I left Tucson to go to Los Angeles, they followed be back there. Back there, we went on the road. My wife modeled clothes. I got some clothes, coats, and suits from a cousin of mine who was at Macy's. They were all dark, black, heavy, interlined. Try to sell that in Hollywood in the summer. So that was the end of the wholesale dress business, and somebody said to us, "For god's sake, you're nice young people here, why don't you open a store and go into the retail end of it?" We opened a store in Sherman Oaks called Country Casuals. It didn't do too badly and then, at this point, the blacklist started to fade.

The writers could work. They could change their names. They could get a front, but they could work. Actors couldn't do it because they had to be on the stage, and neither could the directors. So, under another name—in fact, I had four names; I won't go into it—it was a very amazing situation. The first pseudonymous writing job was *Lassie*. I didn't know what the hell to do with a dog; they'd already been on for a year and a half. I wrote twenty-two of

23

them. Magically, I remembered that there were all kinds of things besides looking for a bone which was a fossil of a mastodon.

Then we did *Daktari, Gilligan's Island, Hitchcock Presents*, and *Rawhide*. I did four *Rawhides*, with Clint Eastwood, and I was given a nice, beautiful bag from the producer, who liked what I was doing, inscribed 'To J.E. Selby,' which was my pseudonym. And when I saw him at the Academy of Motion Picture Arts and Sciences, of which he was a member, I thanked him and said, "Look, I like this bag; I love it and I'm keeping it, but I'm not J. E. Selby. My name is really Bob Lees and I was a blacklisted writer." I'm now telling him after all these years. And he paled. He said, "What do you mean? You didn't have the nerve to tell me that you were blacklisted? Didn't you know that I would have accepted this thing and looked the other way? What kind of a guy do you think I am?"

So these were the kinds of stories of what happened in the blacklist. I don't know if I've gone over my time, but I could tell you a lot more.

STAN

I wanted to ask you about HUAC asking you about your partner, who he was.

ROBERT

All right. That was very interesting. My partner, Fred Rinaldo, who Jean knows, everybody knows very, very well here in this group, didn't need to go to Washington, because after all, he knew he was going to be blacklisted, the lawyers knew he was going to be blacklisted. He didn't want to spend the money on the train and all the lawyers' fees. He just wanted to duck it. So I saw Fred Rinaldo at Wrightwood, where he was in his brother's cabin. We said goodbye to each other, because this was the end of seventeen years of collaboration. That was it; we never collaborated on another picture again. I was through.

When I went to Washington, they asked me, "Who is your collaborator?" I had talked to the attorneys about this beforehand. If they ask me this, and I say, "He's Fred Rinaldo," then they say, "Do you know that Fred Rinaldo is ducking a subpoena?"

and then I'm in terrible trouble. I asked the attorneys what to do and they said, "Take the First Amendment if they ask who your collaborator is." When I asked how I could do that, they just said, "Play it by ear." So when the Committee started asking me, "Who's your collaborator?" I said, "It's on the screen. You know who it is. Why do you ask me who my collaborator is? It's all over the record." They kept after me and after me. Of the hour and a half I was on the stand, fifteen minutes or thirty minutes was taken up with asking about Fred Rinaldo. They knew damn well there was a subpoena out for Fred now, so they really came after me.

So I said, "I think there's something about this man's name that's making me feel very uncomfortable and on this basis, I take the Fifth Amendment. I don't want to incriminate anybody, including myself." And that stopped it. And then they came back with the whole committee, saying things like, "What do you mean? Aren't you proud of your collaborator? You're on the screen with him." I said, "Yes, on the screen. You know where he is." So that was it.

STAN

I have a couple of questions to ask our panel here. This one's for Bernard Gordon, regarding *55 Days At Peking*. Was prolific screenwriter Philip Yordan a front for blacklisted writers?

BERNARD

No, he wasn't a front. He was a man who hired us for cheap money because he could put his name on the script and we worked for a lot less than we would have been working for if we were not blacklisted. So it was very convenient for him and it was damn good for us, because we were getting work which we might not otherwise have gotten. When Dalton Trumbo finally broke the blacklist and the credits were about to be put on the screen for *55 Days at Peking*, I said, "Well the blacklist is over. I want my name on it, not yours," and Yordan said, "Well, that's not possible," because the deal had been made, blah, blah, blah, "but we'll let them put your name on with mine, below mine," and that's how it came out and I'm now fighting with the Guild to get my full credit on that picture as well as on nine others. It happens that I got more credits as a blacklisted writer than anybody else in the guild.

OLIVER

If I might interject something, Bernie is being very modest. He's had a very interesting career. He wound up running a studio in fascist Spain.

STAN

Well, we're going to talk about that, I think, in the third part of our show. Another question is, to all of you, and we have to do it real fast, what percentage of your writing or story lines promoted communist ideology versus story lines of a generalized nature?

BERNARD

That's a joke.

JEAN

That's really a joke.

OLIVER

Do you know, it's a matter of record that a line from a picture called *Tender Comrade,* made by Metro, had the line in it, "Share and share alike, that's democracy," cited as communist propaganda. You had that kind of nonsense. I mentioned the Shirley Temple thing. Eleanor Roosevelt was named. I mean, you can go on and on with this. I'll tell you something else. When I first joined the Party, I was told to read Marx, *The Communist Manifesto.* Well, reading that is like slogging through mud with combat boots on. I don't think anyone has ever gotten through it, you see.

STAN

Robert Lees, what's your comment?

ROBERT

Considering that we did Abbott and Costello, Olsen and Johnson, Martin and Lewis movies, where the communist propaganda came in I don't know, but the producer on Abbott and Costello, when he was called before the Committee—incidentally, he was very reactionary but we liked him, he was a good producer and he liked us —said he had to keep communist propaganda out of Abbott and Costello. Now, I don't know if "Who's on First" had something to do with it, maybe that's 'comspeak,' as they say, but it was pretty ridiculous.

STAN

I have one more question here. You know there are a lot of people out here that are a little young and they don't know about the HUAC/McCarthy years, and this is the question posed from the audience. If you were involved in communism innocently and not breaking the law, why would you be banned from working in Hollywood?

ROBERT

It's very simple and I said it before. We were banned from working in Hollywood by the producers, who were very frightened at the prospect of government action against them. This is very interesting. When the producers went to the Committee and they were friendly witnesses, they were scared to death because they were mostly Jewish. We have to get into this point. There was Mayer, there was Warner, there was Laemmle, and they had a feeling about the Committee being anti-Semitic, which was quite accurate. You should read a book entitled *How the Jews Invented Hollywood*. The producers were anxious to show that they were Americans first and Jewish second.

STAN

You know, Robert, I understand what you're saying and I agree with you, but we're going to have to do that on another show. I have to wrap this up and I want to thank my guests.

OLIVER

I hope so, because we're here at depression prices.

STAN

I want to tell you that our next show will be about how you lived with the blacklist. Ciao, guys, love you, and good night.

THE STANLEY DYRECTOR SHOW

"THE HOLLYWOOD BLACKLIST, PART 3"

06/12/01

Producer/Host
Stanley Dyrector

With Special Guests
JEAN ROUVEROL, BERNARD GORDON
OLIVER CRAWFORD, ROBERT LEES

STAN

Hello, and welcome to our third and final episode of this evening's *Stanley Dyrector Show* with my guests, who are screenwriters. Here's a quick recap on what our other two topics have been: how the panel lived their lives before the blacklist, and on show number two, how they got blacklisted and the effect on their lives.

In this episode, we're going to talk about how their lives changed; how they were able to survive and what they are doing these days—are they making the big bucks?

So, Jean Rouverol, how's by you? Big bucks?

JEAN

No big bucks, in a word. The really good, I thought, Mexican years ended near the end of the '50s. Hugo was feeling weary under the steady grind of work and the major responsibility of six children. And our doctor up north had put him on methedrine, on the assumption that it was non-addictive. Thank you. He was growing increasingly short-tempered with me, the children, and Mexico, generally, but I ignored it. I figured I must be doing something wrong or he wouldn't be so upset. That's when he got a wire from Bob Aldrich, asking him to come to Italy for, quote, "Six-Week Rewrite Biblical Subject." And, sight unseen, he wired off his acceptance.

By now, our oldest two were in college. Once packed, the other four and I followed Hugo to Rome and began a whole new kind of life. The picture proved to be *Sodom and Gomorrah*, and it would be the first picture in more than a decade that Hugo would have his name on. A credit, finally, and it had to be *Sodom and Gomorrah*.

The blacklist was winding to an end, but it had done enormous damage. During our three-and-a-half years in Rome, our marriage also nearly came to an end. Hugo and Trumbo, who had also been put on methedrine, quarreled and for more than a year didn't communicate, although they ended up friends again later. Hugo did a little Jeanne Moreau picture with Joe Losey and we shared credit on a little war picture called *Face In The Rain*, and by late '64, we were on our way home, having spent a year en route in Mexico again, making up our minds whether to go or not. Hugo was soon working for Aldrich again on *The Legend of Lila Claire*, which, late in the assignment, I joined him on.

By now, his mother had died, his father had died, and he was in the throes of what seemed to be a full-fledged breakdown—all in the space of three years—which UCLA had diagnosed as Alzheimer's, incorrectly as we learned later. It was actually arteriosclerotic brain disease. He was undergoing a workup at the Neuropsychiatric Clinic at UCLA in early January of 1968 when he died suddenly of a massive heart
attack at age fifty-three. It would be a long time before the children and I could remember him as he was.

Now I was the children's sole support and living over on Cheremoya in a little apartment. I found my way eventually into soap operas as an associate writer. It had the advantage of providing a steady, if rather modest, income. A literary agent had also started me off on a career of writing young adult non-fiction, getting me little book deals each time I was between soap operas.

The Writers Guild of America/West became my home away from home and I served a few terms on their Board and more than two decades as a Trustee on their Pension and Health Fund. I've also taught soap opera writing and I've written two editions of a book about it. My son has had a thirty-six-year career writing film and television. Two of my daughters have published books and their careers have included teaching, some in college and some in high school, librarianship, court reporting, and marriage and children's counseling.

By and large, we have survived, sometimes even thrived, but not for long. And considering what we've been through, surviving was quite a triumph. The Mexican years, however, are the years that we remember with enormous tenderness and that's mostly what my book is about.

STAN
Thank you, Jean. Bernard, the floor's yours.

BERNARD
Well, while blacklisted, I wrote eight or nine films; some really great ones like *The Zombies of Maura Tau* and *The Man Who Turned to Stone*. I did, however, write some interesting films. One was *The Earth vs. The Flying Saucers*, which has become a cult favorite.

I wrote the first film, actually the only film, that Ronald Reagan and Nancy, then Nancy Davis, starred in together. And in recent years, while he was President, I was interested to watch on television scenes from this picture, finally, with his mouthing the love words that I had written for him to say to Nancy.

But through very good fortune, I ended up in Europe, where I was hired to write *The Day of the Triffids*, which also became a cult favorite. And that got me a contract. I lived three years in Paris and suddenly I had found Hollywood in Madrid, Spain. I then went to Madrid, where I lived in the Hilton Hotel for years on end. I was making two thousand dollars a week. I was writing pictures like *55 Days in Peking, Thin Red Line, Krakatoa East Of*

Java, Custer of the West. And I wound up actually running a small studio outside of Madrid, in a little town called Daganzo, where we made spaghetti westerns and one of the pictures I'm most proud of, and most people don't know, which was *Horror Express*. That's a cult classic which has been largely ignored, but it's an important film.

There I was, living in Madrid, in hotels, going for holidays to Monaco, to St. Moritz, to Rome, Italy, to London, to Paris, and so on. As I said in my book, *Hollywood Exile: or How I Learned to Love the Blacklist*, I really have to admit that I did have a very good time in Europe and I'm very grateful for that whole experience.

But I think it's important to say that this business of communism—and, yes, I was a communist—and whether you agree with me or not is not the issue. The issue is whether you have a right to dissent. There is no meaning to free speech unless it means free speech for people whom you don't agree with. If it's the people you agree with, you don't need the First Amendment.

Now I feel that the whole McCarthy period was a way to destroy dissent in this country and to open the way for the terrible things that happened under American leadership all over the world, starting with Iran, with the Shah, going through all of Africa, Central America, South America, Chile, Argentina. And everywhere, millions and millions of people were killed because of the leadership of the "American Century." And we were people who understood and disagreed and had no chance to speak out because we were blacklisted because of the anti-communist hysteria. And to this day, I think it's important to remember that and to reaffirm it, and to say let's fight for what we think is right.

STAN

I just want to add a footnote to Bernard Gordon's words: The picture he was talking about, with Nancy Reagan and Ronald Reagan, was *Hellcats of the Navy*. So rent it. Oliver Crawford, please tell us your experiences.

OLIVER

Well, I was blacklisted off a picture called *The Kentuckian*. It was the first picture to be directed by and starring Burt Lancaster.

32

I was called in by Harold Hecht, who said he'd just come from a meeting of a subcommittee of the House Un-American Activities Committee, where my name had come up and I would have to do what he did. I'll never forget this. These were his exact words. "You will have to dig a hole, crawl in, and pull the dirt over you if you want to make another quarter in this town."

Well, the long and short of it is, I put my house up for rent, and a subpoena was out for me. I gathered my two kids and in the dark, went to Detroit, where my sister-in-law, who had been a vocalist for Vaughn Monroe and Jimmy Dorsey, took us in. Her husband then rang the ABC radio affiliate in Detroit, where he thought he could bury me in the advertising department. But then he got cold feet and I went to New York, where I found connections, because New York was not as intimidated by the blacklist. They were play-oriented. And the format of live TV in those days, the so-called Golden Age, was oriented to the stage and they had disdain for Hollywood. And through some connections, I got to do *Kraft Theatre* and *Theatre Guild on the Air* at the same time, and a number of shows that kept me going. And my wife, who was a legal secretary, got a part-time job. And I became a house father before it was fashionable as a role reversal, getting two kids off to school and so on. And I got back in a very strange way.

I'd been part of a play and one of the actors, in those days before pornography, used to play the stag circuit. And after the show closed he said, "Ollie, you ever see a stag show?" And I said, "No." He said, "Will your wife let you go?" And my wife said, "You want to see naked ladies? Go." He worked at this place at the St. George Hotel in Brooklyn, where I was introduced to the gals—they were buck naked—and I tried to be blasé about the whole thing, of course. They were very impressed with the fact that I was a Hollywood writer and asked did I know John Wayne or Joan Crawford—I said she was a distant cousin. We went on into this room, which was black save for a spot, and the gals were doing their thing. And all of a sudden, I feel a tap on my shoulder. "Oliver Crawford?" I'm thinking, "The FBI, the FBI caught up with me." He says, "Call home." I figured it was an emergency. I called home and my wife said, "Get home. You just got a call from Lillian

Small"—a prestigious agent at the time—"CBS wants to put you under contract." I said, "What are you talking about?" Well, I had written a play and given it to a friend, Sam Levene—some of you may recall him, a character actor—and he, unbeknownst to me, had sent it to Lillian and she took it to CBS and they were doing a show called *Playhouse 90* and they wanted to put me under contract, which they did, along with Rod Serling, Adrian Spies and Mel Goldberg.

And to this day, I don't know how I got off the blacklist and I don't know who named me. As a matter of fact, many years later, under the Freedom of Information Act, I sent away for my dossier. I got back six pages, all lined and blacked out. I thought, "My God, am I still a threat, after forty years, to the security of the United States?" So very politely, I wrote back and asked for clarification. I got a letter back from the Republican National Committee thanking me for my contribution. That's it. So I figured, to hell with it, let sleeping dogs lie. And that was it.

I had no problem, I resumed a career. I never achieved high celebrity on screenplays. I was always the third or fourth writer called in at a poverty level, to rescue a script when the producer only had $5,000 or $10,000.

Today, of course, all of us—I would guess we have over 320 years, collectively, between us—suffer from ageism. I'll explain: We're dead, we're invisible to people out there. They don't care what we did two years ago, five years ago, forty years ago. If you're a doctor or a lawyer and you build up a background, you're respected for it. Hollywood writers get no respect. So today, when people ask if I'm retired, I say, "No, I'm unemployed; I'm blacklisted again."

STAN

I want to say just one thing about Oliver Crawford. He is a very humble man. There's a story Ollie told me off camera, about his wife telling him, "Ollie, we are not going to rat on our friends. We're going to leave town." And that's what he did. Anyway, Robert Lees, can you add to this mix?

ROBERT

Speaking of ageism, I'll be eighty-nine next month, thank you. So when you talk about surviving, I know what it means. I came to this town in 1930. And I've seen why we are here and I'd like to bring this up, because we have come full circle. We are here in the Samuel Goldwyn Library. Actually it's named for Frances Goldwyn, his widow.

We have been honored by the four talent guilds, who had a great event at the Academy of Motion Picture Arts and Sciences, in which the president of each of the major guilds apologized for what they did not do during the Blacklist period, to those of us who were standing in the front row with badges. UCLA gave us a Lifetime Achievement Award to rival the reward given to Elia Kazan when he was given a Lifetime Achievement award by the Academy, because we had stood up for what we stood up for. Not being outdone by UCLA, or vice versa, USC has put in a magnificent fountain and benches for the Hollywood Ten, a tribute to the blacklist and to the First Amendment, in which many of the things we've said before the Committee are engraved in stone. This is in front of USC.

So we have seen all these things switch. Where before my family in San Francisco, many of them Republicans, wouldn't speak to me—I was the Devil. I am now something of a quote, "I've survived." Abe Polonsky, myself, and Joan Scott were asked by the Museum of Television and Radio to be presented in front of pictures that we have done, TV shows like *Rawhide* and *Hitchcock Presents*, on which I used my pseudonym and Abe Polonsky used his pseudonym on, *You Are There,* and Joan Scott did, at the moment, I can't think quite what her picture was. And they all applauded us for what we have done and they were hoping that maybe they would give the credits on television–which already is being done by the Writers Guild—to give the credits for those people who were blacklisted and under whose names these pictures were written. So it's come full cycle. Everybody is now saying we're okay. There are people who say, "But aren't you Reds?"

The point was, we were Reds—at a time when being Red was being patriotic. And now there's a whole change of what's going on. But one thing has been amazing about this period. The House Un-American Activities Committee, HUAC, and McCarthy, made a thing called the McCarthy period. It's now in the dictionary. People now know there was a period in the United States when free speech was dead. Now they realize when somebody starts to step on you for speaking about it, you can say, "This is what they did in McCarthy's day."

So we are the survivors of the McCarthy period, thank God. We've survived to see it change and the entire switch in Hollywood and why we are here.

STAN

Very well said, Robert. I have a couple of questions from our audience that I want to give our panel: "Did any of your writing during the Blacklist secretly comment on the Blacklist, say in *High Noon*, either in TV or in film?" So who would like to tackle that? Go ahead, Robert.

ROBERT

Very interesting. One of the pictures being done in England was *Robin Hood*, with Richard Greene. And Abe Polonsky wrote for it; Adrian Scott wrote for it; Fred Rinaldo and myself wrote for it. And it was one of these wonderful things, there was no blacklist in England, but we had *Robin Hood*—who was against the King, who was against the Establishment.

You could say anything politically you wanted to say in that period in England, and it was just wonderful and it was one of the great experiences of my life. We wrote for that. There might be other things, but that was where you could do it—in England— and Robin Hood –and a period piece.

STAN

I have a question that says, "Creation or Evolution, why?" I don't understand the question. Does anybody?

BERNARD

We're for evolution.

STAN

Yes, everybody for evolution. Now, "How are your progressive ideals holding up after a lifetime of siege? Are you, each one of you, still political, politically active?"

BERNARD

I'd like to say that now that we have the Bush administration, I'm a little discouraged. I find that there's a real backward movement, that they're destroying so many things we fought for all our lives and the important thing to know—whether you agree with me or not—who doesn't agree with me here? The important thing is to know is that the struggle to make a decent world goes on. The struggle for peace; the struggle for ecology; the struggle for all these things that we know about, that Bush is trying to destroy in the interests of oil and money. That's my opinion. I think my friends here share it. And the important thing is to know that it's not over. It's never over. It's never over. You never win the war—you try to win the battles.

STAN

Okay. Jean Rouverol, did you ever feel like you were a subversive?

JEAN

Good heavens, no. In Mexico, by the way, there's an article in the Constitution, Article 33, that gives the government the right to instantly deport, without even a hearing, just on a *denuncio* of a Mexican citizen, any foreigner who is adjudged to have said or done anything that is denigrate to Mexico. That's why all of these five hundred pages of FBI surveillance of us down in Mexico are so ridiculous. We had to live like nuns and monks. I mean we leaned over backwards never to do one thing that could be construed as radical, publicly.

BERNARD

Imagine how it was living in Franco's Spain.

JEAN

Yeah, worse. We had Saturday morning baseball games, inter-familial, inter-generational. The little kids, their fathers, their mothers, were all playing baseball—and then having brown-bag lunches in our front yard afterwards. We did this for years.

BERNARD

Who won, the Reds or the Whites?

JEAN

It alternated. But wouldn't you know that we learned from those papers, that these baseball games were regularly being reported to the FBI, by their informants, as covers for communist meetings? Honest to Pete.

STAN

You know, Jean, Robert Lees also has something he got from the Freedom of Information Act.

ROBERT

Yes, that's where I got mine from. Look, I have pages and pages.

STAN

Yes. Hold it up, hold it up.

ROBERT

And this is some "Freedom of Information." They don't say *who* told on you, *who* said you did this or that—you can't confront anybody. It's an amazing thing.

One of the things struck me as being rather funny. When I was a Maitre d' in Tucson, Arizona, I thought I was being incognito. But, of course, the FBI was eating at the tables and all the rest of it. And they had already asked the owner of the hotel, and the manager, if they knew anything about me and they said, no they didn't—they just thought I was a very good Maitre d'— which was a total lie. That was really subversive.

STAN

I must add to that, before Jean shows her Freedom of Information Act folder, that Robert Lees, while he was a Maitre d', also had playing in town at the movies, *Abbott and Costello Meets Frankenstein*, while he was in a humble servant's position.

ROBERT

We had two films. We also had *Jumping Jacks* with Martin and Lewis, which incidentally came ten years after it was written because the Writers Guild said, "Well, if you're going to use this much of it," which they had to, "They have to have their names on it."

So here I was, incognito in the dining room, with two films being played on the
main streets.

STAN

And Bernard Gordon, remember, was a producer who could hire actors and writers. And did you hire your friends?

BERNARD

I hired my friend, Julian Zimet, who's sitting here, who wrote—what was it, Julian?

JULIAN ZIMET

Horror Express.

BERNARD

Thank you—and you wrote *Pancho Villa*. And I was very pleased to hire him, and then re-write him, if I wanted to.

STAN

So being a producer had its benefits, naturally. And, all of you guys and doll, are you still writing screenplays right now?

BERNARD

This is what I'm writing.

JEAN

I'm writing a book; I've finished a book. It's published.

STAN

Ollie's got a play; Robert Lees is writing his memoirs.

OLIVER

As a final word, I tell you that, as Bernie says, we're losing again—and we've lost a great deal. We've got to be so damn vigilant because I think we've got a Neandertal government. We don't have a White House Cabinet, we have a boardroom; four ex-CEOs in there, four ex-lobbyists.

STAN

And as we are talking about that, we're on our way out, ladies and gentlemen. And I want to thank you all. Yes, go ahead Ollie.

OLIVER

One last thing. The point is, I can say this today, here in this room and not worry now about Gestapo tactics out there, to stop me.

STAN

That's right, because we are in America, the land of the free and the home of the brave. Am I right Robert Lees?

OLIVER

But we have to keep at it.

ROBERT

You're one hundred percent right and let's keep it that way.

STAN

And let's keep writing comedy. Bob, make us laugh again. And Mr Gordon, make us experience *Day of the Triffids* again.

And Oliver, *Star Trek*, and Jean and I loved *Autumn Leaves*, I gotta tell you, that was one of my favorite movies.

Hey folks, let's give a hand to our great panel here.

Stanley Dyrector, Abraham Polonsky

Chapter Two

THE STANLEY DYRECTOR SHOW

Producer/Host
STANLEY DYRECTOR

Tonight's Guest
ABRAHAM LINCOLN POLONSKY, PART 1
Writer/Director

1999

STAN

Hi, ladies and gentlemen, and welcome to *The Stanley Dyrector Show*. You know, today we are privileged, indeed honored, to have as our guest one of the most renowned writers of our generation, of the world really. His name: Abraham Lincoln Polonsky. What a name, what a guy. Let me tell you something about Mr. Polonsky. Mr. Polonsky wrote the films – actually he wrote *Body and Soul,* and that movie was with John Garfield, if you recall. But he also wrote another movie with John Garfield, called *Force of Evil*, which, by the way, Martin Scorsese said was an inspiration to him for all of the films that he has done about those wise guys. And I'll tell you something else: Mr. Polonsky also wrote *Odds Against Tomorrow*, with Harry Belafonte. And Robert Wise, the film director, said that Mr. Polonsky wrote that movie when Mr. Polonsky was blacklisted, you know. Mr. Polonsky also wrote

Madigan; he also wrote *I Can Get it for You Wholesale.* He's written novels. He was one of the writers of the CBS television series *You Are There*, that Walter Cronkite narrated. And I guess I'm kind of overjoyed by the fact that I have Mr. Polonsky with us right now.

ABE

Which of those movies did I direct?

STAN

Which of those movies did Mr. Abraham Polonsky direct? Actually, I didn't mention *Tell Them Willie Boy Is Here*, because Mr. Polonsky directed *Tell Them Willie Boy Is Here*. He also directed *Force of Evil* with John Garfield and Thomas Gomez. Am I right or wrong?

ABE

You're almost right.

STAN

Almost right. But look, I'm doing all the dialogue. You're the man who writes that dialogue. Can you talk to us a little bit, Abraham?

ABE

About what?

STAN

How did you become Abraham Lincoln Polonsky?

ABE

Because my father was insane. He had a nice name like Henry, so he called me Abraham Lincoln. And the kids in school called me "Father Abraham." So I come back and I tell my father, "Why did you do this to me?" And he said, "Some day you'll appreciate it." I'm now eighty-eight years old. I still haven't appreciated it.

STAN

Well, look, you're much younger than eighty-eight. You're kind of putting us on. I mean, I can't really believe that you're eighty-eight years old.

ABE

Shall I show you my birth certificate? I happened to bring it along.

STAN

No, actually – I know you're over twenty-one. But tell me something.

ABE

What?

STAN

The first thing that you wrote – you were kind of an inspired kid – I guess the muses were hanging over your head. Didn't you write something about Don Quixote's helmet when you were a kid?

ABE

How do you know that?

STAN

How do I know that? I'm Stan. I'm the guy doing the interview.

ABE

I was nine years old.

STAN

Really. And was that the reason you became a writer, because you wrote about Don Quixote's helmet?

ABE

Nope. I became a writer because my mother, as I was being born said, "What else can the son of a bitch do?" She said, "Well, he can write. Anybody can write." That's how I became a writer.

STAN

Is that right? I'll bet your father was pretty proud of you.

ABE

Never.

STAN

Never was proud of you? Very good.

ABE

But the three old men on the block liked me. *(members of organized crime)

STAN

Three old men on the block liked you?

ABE

Yes.

STAN

Is this the block in Manhattan on the lower East Side?

ABE

Yes.

STAN

Can you tell us a little bit more about your little job – you worked for your father,
right?

ABE

I got up every morning. I washed the floor of the drug store; I dusted everything, took in the mail, and then took a hypodermic of cocaine to be in a good mood for the rest of the day. So what do you want to know?

STAN

Well, I want to know, didn't a couple of gavones steal from your father's pharmacy?

ABE

It was during Prohibition time. And one night, one day when I came to work in the morning, I saw the store had been robbed and in those days, the doctors had the prescriptions given to them by the government. And they could write a prescription for about a pint of bonded booze, whiskey, because that's the kind they had. And that's in the National Formulary, which is the book that contains the kind of medicines that are legitimate – and booze is in there, naturally. So anyway, it was all stolen when I came into the store. My father was upset by it, of course, 'cause that meant that the government would soon be interested in coming around that store and finding out about this and that.

So the three old men used to hang around on the corner and take their hats off every time a hearse went by; they were just a block away from the church, they showed their respect. So they said, "Don't do anything, Doc. We'll take care of it." And a week later, on another day when I came in to wash up as usual, there was all the whiskey, still in the cases, and there was also some stuff he took from a case where we kept the cocaine, morphine – all that kind of stuff that they used to prescribe. And when my father came in, he was very happy of course. And the three old men came in and said, "Everything okay?" My father thanked them and then one of the old men said, "You know, the fellow who did this wants to apologize." My father said, "It's not necessary. I'm glad I have it back." And the old man said, "He really wants to apologize." So my father said, "Well, I'll be in all next week in the afternoons and I'll be in the week after, and let him come in." And they say, "Well, he has to get out of the hospital first." If, indeed, he ever got out. 'Cause I never saw him.

STAN

You know, you speak pretty good Sicilian, too.

ABE

Pourquoi non? Je parle français aussi.

STAN

Is that Italian or is that French?

ABE

French.

STAN

You speak all kinds of languages.

ABE

As long as it's not English.

STAN

As long as it's not English.

ABE

That's why I write in English. It's the only language I can't speak.

STAN

That's the only language you can't speak! Abraham, did you immediately come out to Hollywood as a writer? How did your career start?

ABE

Life went on, as it does. And I graduated from college of the City of New York and was appointed to the faculty, in the English Department, where I taught English Literature and writing and stuff like that. And meanwhile, I went to Columbia Law School and I was graduated from there also, and I passed the Bar and I got a job in a law office. And one of the senior partners was related to a woman by the name of Gertrude Berg, who had a radio series called *The Goldbergs*.

STAN

The Goldbergs, I remember that one.

ABE

And she came in one day and said to the senior partner, "I want to do part of the series on a law case," and of course I, being the last one hired in the law firm, was given the honor of being introduced to her. She was a kind of plumpish, nice looking woman, very smart, who wrote, directed, produced and acted in her show, and they said, "Polonsky will help you." So we went to my office and I started explaining the laws of evidence and things like that. In about two seconds, I could see the blur come into her face, then her eyes glazed over and she was out. So I knew it was a waste of time. She didn't know I was a writer. So I said, "Well, what's the story?" So this she could tell me. I said, "Well, what's the first episode you want to do?" 'Cause I had never seen her show. After all, a young man of my age is not about to watch serials in the daytime, right?

STAN

Right. You're into better things.

ABE

Not better things – I'm working. So she told me the plot. So I called in the secretary and I dictated it, the whole story as she told it to me. And then I said to her, "All you have to do is change the dialogue, which has nothing to do with law. Leave the law stuff alone. And you'll be right on the law and it will sound like you." And she thanked me very much and the next morning I got a check for fifty dollars, which was like a million in those days 'cause on both my jobs I didn't earn fifty dollars a week.

STAN

Wow, that is something. Did you go right into movies right after that?

49

ABE

Oh, no. So let's continue this story?

STAN

Yes, sure.

ABE

We've got hours, right, to kill?

STAN

Yes, sure.

ABE

So Berg comes in the next day. Of course, there's a second episode. There's an episode a day. They were fifteen-minute episodes in those days. And she said, "We have to do the second one." I said, "I'll be happy to help you 'cause I'm very grateful for the fifty dollars, but I have to go to court," because we represented the dyeing and printing of textile industry and we had a lot of cases. If a dress dye ran, you think they gave the woman her fifty dollars back? No way. She had to go to court. So they defended every case and of course I as the least important person had all those cases. So I was in court a lot. So she said, "I'll take care of it." And she went and spoke to the senior partner and he called me in and said, "Abe, go with her and do whatever she likes and come back after you're through. We want you here and we'll get someone else to do your job. But we'll pay you."

STAN

Well that's good.

ABE

So, Mrs. Berg lived on Central Park West at the Majestic, on two floors, with her servants, her children, her husband, who was an engineer in the sugar industry, and her father, who was a retired hotel operator from the Catskills. And I'd come over there, walk across the Park, 'cause I lived on the other side, and I'd meet her and we'd discuss her stuff and I helped her as much as she wanted me to help her, and the first week I get a check for two hundred and fifty dollars.

STAN

Wow!

ABE

After I fainted, of course. And after I got up, I said, "What's going on here?" She said, "Well, they're paying you what? Nothing. I'm paying you a minimum amount for the work you do. I'm giving you two hundred fifty dollars a week, is that okay?" I said, "Yeah, I can buy a Rolls Royce." Anyhow, so there I was then, earning two hundred and fifty dollars a week, doing this stuff. In those old days, aside from Shirley Temple, there was little boy called Bobby Breen. He had a beautiful voice and he was the male equivalent of Shirley Temple, making the same kind of movies, and she was hired to write the screenplay of a Bobby Breen movie in between seasons. And she said to me, "Would you like to come to Los Angeles with me?" I said, "Do I have to?" She said, "It would be very nice if you did, and of course we'll pay you more money." You can't believe how incredible all these numbers were to me, 'cause I knew that fifteen dollars a week was a lot of money. So my wife and I, I was married then, my wife and I went to California. You take the 20th Century to Chicago and then you change trains and it's two days and two nights, I think, and we end up in California and Berg was there and she got me a place to live on the Sunset Boulevard, an apartment, nice, and we went to work on the screenplay. Meanwhile, I was in a different kind of world altogether.

STAN

Right.

ABE

And the more I saw of it, the more I was sure I never wanted to have anything to do with it.

STAN

Really?

ABE

Of course. There's nothing more horrible than the movies. But I did manage to meet Ernest Hemingway and so on. They were raising money for ambulances for Spain in those days, the Spanish Civil War. And in fact, I saw Gypsy Rose Lee do one of her shows and the money was dedicated to the ambulances in Spain but the clothes were dedicated to a second-hand dealer some place. Anyhow, it was charming. And then a comedian by the name of Blue, he did a striptease too.

STAN

Ben Blue, was it?

ABE

Yeah. He did a striptease too. But there were no secrets. After all, I recognized all the parts, whereas in the case of Gypsy Rose Lee, I wondered did anybody have parts like that? So there I was in Hollywood and then it was over. So we came back East and I still worked for Gertrude Berg, 'cause she didn't want to let me go and I didn't want to be let go cause I'd walk over in the morning, do the scene with her, what we had to do, and then the rest of the day belonged to me and I could go home and write, 'cause I'm writing a novel all this while. 'Cause I am a writer, self-elected, but I am a writer. And then I wrote a book, which got published, and all that stuff. And I never thought of going out to Hollywood. And now I'll skip a lot. It's now World War Two.

STAN

World War Two, okay.

ABE

And I am a member of the OSS.

STAN

The Office of Strategic Services. I was able to say it right?

ABE

Not bad for an immature humorist – and so, it's a week before I'm going overseas and they've sent me home to say goodbye to my wife and all the rest of this stuff.

But meanwhile, I'm sitting in the office in Washington and in walks a young lady and I think her name was Meta Rosenberg and she was working for Paramount Pictures and she gives me a contract at Paramount Pictures, a five-year contract, starting at two hundred and fifty dollars a week and going up to enormous sums (to me), but they had a yearly option to renew or not renew. So I immediately signed this, although I was leaving the next week and I was supposed to report to Hollywood the next week, and then I went to General Donovan and told him what I did. Because in those days, if you had a contract to work anyplace, and you had to go overseas, they had to fulfill it when you came back, if you were lucky enough to come back. So in other words I had a job guaranteed at Paramount, and that's the reason I signed it. And then Donovan sent me out to the Coast; I went by an Army plane.

STAN

This was Wild Bill Donovan, right, that's what he was called?

ABE

Yes. He sent me out to the Coast in a military plane and with a letter addressed to Paramount, telling them to use me and announce that I was working for them, and they were sending me to London to cover the air war in a documentary. That was my cover story, which was more interesting than my real life, but what's the difference? So that's what happened. I came back and then I walked in after the war, which I came back from, by the way. This may seem odd to you, but I managed to do that.

STAN

No, it doesn't seem odd. You had mentioned that you had some very, very close friends that did not come back from the war.

ABE

Well, they did not make the deal with the devil that I did, which was to sign a Hollywood contract. If you make a deal with the devil, the devil takes care of you. It's the only way that I can account for the difference.

STAN

Well, you wrote *Body and Soul.*

ABE

Wait a minute. I'm at Paramount.

STAN

Okay, you're at Paramount.

ABE

So they asked me to do a picture. I do a picture called, something about – it was a picture with Marlene Dietrich.

STAN

Called *Golden Earrings.* "There's a story the gypsies know . . ."

ABE

So she's in *Golden Earrings* and so's Ray Milland in it, and the story is about a captain, a colonel, in the Army Air Force who gets dumped into Germany, hides with the gypsies. Little does he know that the gypsies are the first into the concentration camps, and of course that's the plot. So that's what I write and I look up the Romany language and how the gypsies talk and their customs and all that stuff. And I write it. And of course then the man producing it, who was a writer also, he rewrote it and made it into a comedy.

STAN

A real writer's nightmare.

ABE

'Cause I know when I went to the movies, I only last ten minutes and I walked out. But I did have an honor out of that though.

STAN

Oh, what was the honor?

ABE

I went on the set one day and Marlene Dietrich said to me, "You wrote this picture?" I said, "I wrote some of it," and she said, "That's worth a kiss, isn't it?," and she kisses me on the cheek and I said to her, "Miss Dietrich, a kiss on the cheek from Marlene Dietrich is an insult." She said, "What do you want?" I said, "A Marlene Dietrich kiss." The next minute, I was on the floor and she's on top of me and, well, she's giving me a Marlene Dietrich kiss. It took me about two years to recover from it. Anyhow, that's my memory of *Golden Earrings*. Which is not bad.

STAN

That's terrific.

ABE

But of course we never could get another picture made and a friend of mine – they're always turning you down for one reason or another – and then a friend of mine, Arnold Manoff, who was working over at a new little studio two blocks away from Paramount, called, what was the name of it?

STAN

Two blocks away from Paramount? Well, there was Raleigh Studio, but that was later on, I think.

ABE

I'll remember it. So anyhow—he was working with John Garfield over there and they had a bunch of stars there, including— well, the very biggest stars – it was like a new United Artists and that's what they were trying to found, because Loew, Jr. was in charge, and Charlie Einfeld, formerly Vice President of . . .

STAN

It was Allied Artists.

ABE

No, it wasn't Allied Artists.

STAN

RKO?

ABE

No. Well, I'll remember it shortly. Anyhow, so Manoff told me about this thing. And I said to Manoff, "I'm gonna go to New York. To hell with this stuff. I'll give up this contract. It's no fun working here. They never make the pictures." So he says, "Wait a minute," and he calls up Garfield and he speaks to him and says, "You know Polonsky?" We had met. He says, "Well, he's got a boxing story that'll kill you." And Garfield says, "Come over then." The studio we have to go to is two blocks away from Paramount. I have no story at all. We're walking along the street and I say, "What am I gonna do?" He says, "Work on something." Well, by the time we get to our studio there and Garfield, we met and talked and Roberts was there, as producer and a partner, and I told the story and they loved it. So Garfield said to me, "Can you stay another hour here?" I said, "Yes." He says, "You stay another hour and we're calling a meeting and I want you tell the story to the head of the studio, the head of production and all the different people here, so they'll know what we're working on." So while he's away, I'm working on the story now. And we have this meeting in David Loew's office and they're all sitting around. And so I tell the story and since I'm showing off, it's working. And when I get through, they're all enthusiastic. At which point, I am told, I went to the door and started to leave, and Charlie Einfeld says, "Where are you going, Abe? We want you to write the story." And I said,

"But I'm under contract to Paramount Pictures. Get yourself a writer." And I closed the door and left. It was an interesting drama. I knew what would happen. As I arrived at the main gate at Paramount, the man there knew me. He said, "Abe, they want you in the main office." And so I went to the main office and saw the head of the studio, I think the man's name was Ginsberg, or something, at that time. And he said, "We just lent you to John Garfield as a writer, to do a picture. We'll pay your salary. But we made a contract. We're getting a thousand dollars a week for you." I said, "You mean I'm not getting the thousand dollars?" They said," No." I said, "I'm not gonna do it. You don't think I'm gonna work and you're gonna collect money on me?" I said, "That's not the way I think of this business, so I'll just stay here at Paramount. You want to fire me, fire me."

STAN

They didn't fire you. I know they didn't fire you.

ABE

They paid the money. They paid the money. And suddenly I was one of the highest-priced writers in town and I hadn't written the screenplay yet. And then I realized this is a crazy business.

STAN

Yeah, it is.

ABE

Idiots, maniacs, fools.

STAN

Abraham, do you know that we have probably about a minute left, if that, of our time. You're so compelling. We have to do another show on another day.

ABE

Where? In Siam?

STAN

We're gonna do another show in Siam. We're gonna keep talking, and I love you, Abraham Lincoln Polonsky. How could Congressman Joseph Veller...

ABE

Velde.

STAN

Velde, say that you were the most dangerous man in America? How could this guy say that? You're the most dangerous man in America? You were an OSS man, but that isn't why he said it.

ABE

You want to hear it or not? You got time now?

STAN

Well, as the credits roll. I don't know if we do have the time.

ABE

No, you don't. It's a long story.

STAN

Okay, so we're gonna do it at another time.

ABE

You mean I have to see you again?

STAN

Well, sure, I'm not such a bad guy.

ABE

It's very boring.

STAN

I'm gonna pay you overtime, double time.

ABE

What's double zero?   Shall I tell you what happened?

STAN

Tell me what happened.

ABE

So Velde, when I appeared before Velde...

STAN

House Un-American Activities Committee?

ABE

And he was a former FBI agent, but he represented something in Chicago.

THE STANLEY DYRECTOR SHOW

Producer/Host
STANLEY DYRECTOR

Tonight's Guest
ABRAHAM LINCOLN POLONSKY, PART 2
Writer/Director

[1999]

STAN

Hi, ladies and gentlemen, welcome once again to The Stanley Dyrector Show. We are indeed privileged and honored to have Part Two of our interview with Mister Abraham Lincoln Polonsky, writer and director. Let me backtrack for a minute from our last show. The name of that studio you went to see John Garfield at, where you got the writing job for *Body and Soul,* was Enterprise Studios.

You were nominated for an Academy Award for that movie.

ABE

So what?

STAN

Well, that kind of made you a little more bankable, right, as a Hollywood writer?

ABE

Who wanted to be bankable?

STAN

You didn't want to be bankable?

ABE

No, what am I, a car? I have to be bankable?

STAN

You're right; you're a human being.

ABE

I'm an artist.

STAN

Bravo. Right on.

ABE

I think.

STAN

I think you are an artist. But in Hollywood, they are very commercial in their thinking. So didn't that kind of hold you in good stead with these moguls?

ABE

Well, they treated me with the lack of respect that I expected, so it was fine. When we shot the picture we had a great cameraman, James Wong Howe.

STAN

Awesome. James Wong Howe.

ABE

And we had a great cast.

STAN

Anne Revere I know was in it.

ABE

Well, name the cast.

STAN

Name the cast? I can't even remember my own name – much less name the cast.

ABE

Who am I being interviewed by, a passing stranger?

STAN

Charlie Rose. But go ahead.

ABE

Anyhow, the picture was well cast. And when they shot it, I went every day.

STAN

You went every day? They allowed the writer on the set?

ABE

What do you mean, the writer on the set? I could fire anybody I liked, because I'm now representing Garfield. So I went through the whole thing, with the editing and everything, and when I got through, Garfield said, "If you want to direct the next picture, you can."

STAN

Really?

ABE

Yeah. So I said, "I never went to a summer camp, you know. I never directed anybody." And he says, "Well, if you want to direct you can. All it has to be is be a meller," which is an abbreviation for a melodrama. You may not understand the technical language of the studios.

STAN

I didn't know that you were an auteur.

ABE

A what?

STAN

You were going to be a writer/director. That's the ultimate, isn't it?

ABE

No, the ultimate is to own the studio and to have a pretty girl, living on the beach. That's the ultimate, as I gathered from when I worked there. In any event, the next picture, I remember the book, which I read.

STAN

That was *Force of Evil*, right?

ABE

Yeah.

STAN

That was a best seller, wasn't it, *Force of Evil*, about the mob?

ABE

It was a book called *Tucker's People* by. . .

STAN

By Ira somebody.

ABE

Ira Wolfert. So I told Garfield the plot. It was about the numbers racket. And he says, "That's great, buy the book." So I went to New York; I had a conference with Ira and I said, "Come out and we'll work it out," 'cause the book is very thick. This was only going to be a regular picture, you know. My friend Donald Ogden Stewart, who was living in London at the time, still had a house at the beach and he had a cook who lived there too. So the author of the book lived there and I went out there every day and we walked on the beach and we skimmed the characters and we decided on the plot. And then we were through and I said, "Now go back and write a screenplay," which he couldn't do, of course. I said, "I wouldn't use a word of it, don't worry. I'm writing my own screenplay." But I gave him a credit anyhow, because after all I'm the author and director. So that became *Force of Evil*.

STAN

I recall when I saw *Force of Evil*, I rented it from one of those infamous places that rent videos. Martin Scorsese did the opening, the introduction, and said that your films, in particular one of them, *Force of Evil*, was an inspiration to him to write his wise-guy movies. I thought that was a very terrific compliment, coming from one of America's great film makers. How do you feel about it?

ABE

Well, I didn't know him, so I thought it was a compliment.

STAN

You didn't pay him off, then?

ABE

I paid him off later. In any event that was an interesting experience, directing a picture.

STAN

Thomas Gomez played his brother, Garfield's brother. And that was a very, very unique movie. It looked like you filmed a great deal of it in Manhattan.

ABE

We did. Started on Wall Street and ended up under the bridge.

STAN

Is that right? In the film, Thomas Gomez's body is on the rocks, down by the river.

ABE

In the book he gets killed, but that's not the way. You see, movies are made up of images—you know that—and therefore how you use them aesthetically and put them together is where the technique comes in, and where the art comes in. Because these images are collected and you move from one to another and how you move from one to another are the language of film. And if you don't know that language, everything is silly. I always cut from feeling to feeling, not from central image to central image, and so it works very well.

STAN

But where did you acquire that knowledge, since it was the first film that you were going to direct?

ABE

Did you ever hear of God?

STAN

God looks over Abraham Polonsky's shoulder.

ABE

Whenever I needed something, I called him and he gave me an answer. I'm God's promised child.

STAN

In other words, were you inspired by other film makers?

ABE

Yes.

STAN

By whom, might I ask?

ABE

Jean Vigo.

STAN

I'm not familiar with him.

ABE

He was a French director and he did two famous pictures, which was all he did before he died, and I thought he was wonderful, so I was influenced by him a little bit. And also, remember, I been going to the movies ever since I been a baby. Any American's life story was how he went to the movies every week, right?

STAN

Sure.

ABE

I went to the movies every week. I even remember Theda Bara.

STAN

Really?

ABE

Yeah.

STAN

You have the memory of an elephant.

ABE

Is that a compliment?

STAN

Since *Force of Evil* was a very good experience, how about the other films that you directed, like *Tell Them Willie Boy Is Here?*

ABE

Which I directed eighteen years after I was blacklisted.

STAN

So what happened, how did the blacklist come about?

ABE

The blacklist came about because Harry Truman was conducting a war with Joe Stalin about who was going to run Central Europe. And with the House Committee and McCarthyism and so on, since the Russians were ostensibly called communists, everybody who was a left-winger of some kind was called a communist. And when they called you before the House Committee, they asked you, "Who are your friends?" Now everybody doesn't have the honorable character of a certain man— who's now being given a special award by the Academy because he's a stool pigeon—he's getting the stool pigeon award, which was formerly known as the snitch-and-tell award, you know.

STAN

You were a member of the OSS. This is what I don't understand. You were a member of the Office of Strategic Services, and that became the CIA. Now how the heck can they have the nerve to say that you were an enemy, like you were the one of the most dangerous people in America, as Congressman Joseph Velde said, how the hell can they come off to say that about you?

ABE

Well there was a guy from the CIA there and when Velde was threatening me, because whenever they asked me questions, I said, "I won't tell you who the members of the OSS were that I worked with," and they were threatening me with jail and this and that, because I didn't stand on anything, I didn't take the Fifth or the First Amendment, anything, I said, "I'm not going to tell you," because it was a military secret. And the guy from the CIA came up and spoke to the Chairman, who spoke to the congressman and shut him up. And the congressman was so furious that he said as he exited, "You're the most dangerous man in America," and that was in all the papers, and when I got home my wife said, "They found you out," but I think she meant something else. What do you want to know?

STAN

Well, I want to know how long did that blacklist last?

ABE

Eighteen years. For eighteen years, I had to write using fronts, pseudonyms, and so on. But I was able to work.

STAN

You were able to work, but didn't Hoover also take away your passport to travel?

ABE

Yeah.

STAN

So you couldn't go overseas.

ABE

I didn't want to.

STAN

You didn't want to go overseas?

ABE

No. When I wanted to go overseas, I did.

STAN

I heard a story, or I read somewhere, that somehow you made more money when you were blacklisted than you did when you were not blacklisted.

ABE

I finally raised the price. Everybody wanted me to work for them, so what I did was charge them more.

STAN

So who were some of your fronts, or what were their names?

ABE

I can't tell you things like that.

STAN

Why can't tell me things like that?

ABE

They're the ones who can tell you. I can't tell you that; I keep our arrangement. And since they're lucky enough to be dead, there's no one going to find out.

STAN

But I also read that you also paid the income tax of the fronts.

ABE

Yes. I paid the income tax of all these things because once you're straight with the income tax, they never snitch. And that's how the mob gets on, they pay their taxes. They don't pay their taxes, then the government gets after them.

STAN

There's a phrase I want to get to. I recall Walter Cronkite saying, on the television show *You Are There*, this is what he said: "What sort of a day was it? A day like all days, filled with those

events that alter and illuminate our time. And you are there."
That's your line.

ABE

I know, but you don't say it the way he did. He said it
like it was news. You say it like you're making a speech on a street
corner for a bum who shouldn't get elected.

STAN

So how did you come up with those lines?

ABE

Did you read what Sidney Lumet said?

STAN

Sidney Lumet said that you could write, you could make
melodies out of the language. You could write and it would appear
in your writing as if you were born in France or England or in
the old days. Because for *You Are There*, you wrote stories in many
instances about the old, ancient days and it was like an ancient
writing these teleplays. Now either you're the reincarnation of
some ancient bard or Abraham Polonsky.

ABE

When Shakespeare quit, he called me and he said, "Abe,
I have a lesson for you, don't get involved with writing a new play
or a new show every week or two weeks; that drives you crazy.
That's why I quit and left and I never wrote a line of poetry again,
because I thought of those actors waiting and I couldn't stand it."
So I was inspired by his call and I decided that if he could do it,
then I could do it.

STAN

But you must have read all of those guys.

ABE

You're talking to someone who was appointed to the
faculty of City College of New York when he was graduated. I

was appointed to the English Department. And I also went to Columbia Law School. I'm an educated person, I'm sorry to say.

STAN

You are Professor Abraham Lincoln Polonsky then.

ABE

I am, at USC.

STAN

Indeed, I am quite privileged to sit here and talk with you, Abraham.

ABE

You are more privileged than you think because I feel like leaving. What else do you want to know? Listen, we could talk for hours, you know. The story of my life takes up a whole life. So we can't waste time here.

STAN

Well, we're not wasting time. This is all really valuable. It was Robert Wise who said you wrote that script for *Odds Against Tomorrow*.

ABE

That's true. A lawyer that I knew and Harry Belafonte knew—I was blacklisted, living in New York—introduced Harry to me. And Harry came and had this story that he bought about a heist and it involved three men: an ex-cop, a white guy, and a black man. And their relationship and the bank job they pull off is destroyed by the fact of the prejudice of the white man for the black man. And it was gorgeously acted and Harry was gorgeous in it. And the director did a lovely job on it, except he made it too long. It's okay.

STAN

So your blacklisted days ended when you took over the film *Madigan* from Howard Rodman, is that true?

ABE

Well, Howard Rodman was working for a producer by the name of Rosenberg. And Rosenberg had a very bad habit. He had a bowl on his desk and in this bowl are pencils with sharp points, and when he sees a script, he immediately takes a pencil as if, even without reading it, he knows he has to fix it. And his idea of fixing a script is to put in all the scenes that the author leaves out because you don't need them. Like, for instance, if I'm shooting a story and I want to give our conversation, I just cut to it. But the way Rosenberg would do it, he would write the following: "Have a cigarette? Lights it. How's your mother? Great." And there's a little conversation first and then he says, "Listen, I want to ask you to kill somebody." So I used to leave out everything except, "I want you to kill somebody." But the point about it is that Rosenberg got Howard Rodman so sore, he wouldn't work for him anymore. So Rosenberg came to me in New York and tried to hire me to do a series on the OSS. And I turned him down because I was making so much money I didn't need him. And he said, "But it'll get you off the blacklist." So I said, "In that case, I'll be out on the next plane." And I came out there and when my name was submitted to NBC, they said, "Get somebody else." Whereupon Jennings Lang, from Universal, called them up and said, "Are you telling me who I'm going to get to write the shows?," using some language which we can't repeat here.

STAN

You can say whatever you want on this show.

ABE

Yeah, but it's not nice. It's not nice to hear Jennings Lang say to the head of NBC, "Go fuck yourself." That's not nice, it shouldn't be said. Some little girl might hear it.

STAN

Our audience is mature, but go ahead further.

73

ABE

I think it refers to a social custom that you should get used to.

STAN

So that led to *Tell Them Willie Boy Is Here* then?

ABE

Yes.

STAN

So, in other words, Universal actually lifted the blacklist from you?

ABE

Yes.

STAN

So it was somebody like Lew Wasserman?

ABE

I knew Lew, he was the agent for John Garfield when I first met him, and he's an honest man and his word can be trusted. Just like Zanuck. The others, I'm not so sure.

STAN

But these were the real. . .

ABE

When they said something, they did it.

STAN

Like Harry Cohn, in those old days?

ABE

Well, Harry Cohn would do what he felt like, not necessarily what he promised.

STAN

Oh, I see.

ABE

But these two were different – and Wasserman especially. He's a gentleman, he's a scholar and he reads all the scripts.

STAN

Really?

ABE

He may even be a judge of good whiskey, I don't know.

STAN

Abe, I wanted to ask you: was, or is there, a film you would like to get off the ground?

ABE

Well, I tried to. I actually invested my own money in it, against my wife's wishes. She says, "Anything that you pay for, they won't do." She has a rule. She's never wrong about anything and she's right about that too. It was *Mario, The Magician*, by Thomas Mann and I wanted to do that and I wrote the screenplay and everything. And I was paying Thomas Mann money for the rights to do it.

STAN

Was he living here in California at the time?

ABE

Yes, at that time, it was when he was living in California before he went back to Germany. That was during the war. In any event, I never made it. And I never made it because of the reason that my wife said. The moguls really should be involved in an enterprise in which they sell fish, you see, and not movies, which are works of art. They're in the fish business, as you can tell.

STAN

Well, you know, Abraham, do you realize that our time, again, has passed us by here.

ABE

When you talk to me, time will pass all the time, because I can sit here and talk for the next three to four years, and that's the way I could extend my life. Since I'm eighty-eight now, if I talk for three to four years, I could get a little older.

STAN

So maybe you would give us the great pleasure of doing another show with us.

ABE

If you're foolish enough to ask me, I may do it.

STAN

I'd really want to do it because I think we'd all like to know more about you, more about your life.

ABE

Like to hear about my underground activities in France?

STAN

Of course I want to hear about that.

ABE

I was there for the liberation of Paris.

STAN

Well, that is going to be on another one of our shows.

ABE

No.

STAN

Come one, give the troops a break. I want to say, my friend, Abraham Polonsky, I love this guy, this man is a beautiful gentleman.

ABE

I want to thank you for your enthusiasm and lack of understanding.

STAN

And we're going to just keep on talking as our director takes us out so gently into the night.

Richard Powell

Chapter Three

Stanley Dyrector's Senior Prom

1994

Tonight's Guest
RICHARD POWELL
Writer/Producer

STAN

Hi, ladies and gentlemen, and welcome to *Senior Prom*. I'm your host, Stanley Dyrector. My guest, writer-producer Richard Powell, is highly regarded among his peers in the film and television industry. This multi-talented writer was born in Cincinnati, Ohio. I won't hold that against you, Richard. He's known as a superb craftsman for his comedy and dramatic expertise. He's written for newspapers, radio, TV, and films. It should be noted he's also a veteran of two fronts of action: one as a soldier in World War II, where he rose from the rank of private to captain; and in another battle, the trenches of the Hollywood wars, where he was a blacklisted writer who had to use a pseudonym and take less money for his work. In the Writers Guild of America/West union activities, Richard Powell was also President of the TV/Radio Branch. In 1994 he received from the Guild the prestigious Morgan Cox Award. Due to time constraints, we can't list all of his 250 credits. Here's a handful: *Life of Riley*, starring William Bendix; *I Married Joan*, starring Joan Davis; *Topper*—I loved that one; the *Richard Diamond* show, starring Richard Powell, the actor; Bob Hope and Lucille Ball's Specials; *Hogan's Heroes*, for

79

which Richard wrote the shooting script for the pilot. So, Richard, tell our intellectual audience, how did you become a writer?

RICHARD

Well, I guess it was because I came into the world as kind of a pudgy kid with no aptitude for sports. So I read and I read a lot. I read and devoured short stories from magazines. I loved them. I didn't realize at the time that I was going to be using those later on, not that I stole, you understand, I adapted. But those were the resources on which I drew later on.

STAN

You were in the Army when you became a writer, or was this prior?

RICHARD

Well, I went to college and I was a writer in the campus newspaper. I had my own column in which I gave everybody hell, which was a lot of fun. I wanted to be a newspaperman when I got out of college, but I couldn't get anybody to read my material.

So I went into radio. I'd done some radio in college. I worked for a small station and I was just getting started, I thought, when I got drafted. This was right after the start of World War II. I was in the Army four years. I came back to Cincinnati and worked for a while at the same radio station. Then somebody did me a great favor and fired me, so I set my sails for California. I came out here in my ten-year-old Plymouth, with $1,500 courtesy of the Army poker games.

STAN

You were a gambler in the Army, a hustler?

RICHARD

I wasn't exactly a hustler. I started out as a loser. My early training came back to me and I went out and bought a book. And from then on it was all easy, because nobody else in the Army ever read a book about poker. So that's what I came out on.

STAN

That's very adventurous. So you came out to California and you had some mad money from your poker games to keep you going. How long did it take you to become a big time writer?

RICHARD

It took me about a year to become anything. Again I had trouble getting people to read my material. Except one man, and he worked at the unemployment office and every six weeks he had to interview me to make sure that I was taking steps in my chosen profession. So I showed him my material and he thought it was great. But for a long time, he was the only one. I did find out that Edgar Bergen, who had a radio program at that time, would read the work of new writers. He was one of the few. So I quickly wrote out some material which I thought would go in his program and I waited and I waited and I waited. After three months, I finally got a letter and I opened it up, I was all charged up, and the letter said, "Every month I read the work of perhaps three hundred aspiring writers. Out of these, I generally pick about five who I think will be ready for professional work. Unhappily, you are not one of that number." But he was nice. He said, "My constructive advice is, write your jokes funnier and closer together." So there I was. My money was running out and my confidence was running out. And then one night, in the little apartment I had in downtown Los Angeles, I got a telegram from New York, a program to which I'd sent some material, and they wanted to buy the material for a show; five hundred dollars.

STAN

Wow, the check was in the mail? That is a Hollywood story.

RICHARD

That enabled me to get an agent and from the agent, I got a job on *Life of Riley*, with William Bendix, and I was on there for two years.

STAN

Writing probably one of my favorite characters, Digby O'Dell, the friendly undertaker. And Peg was Riley's wife's name. That was a wonderful show.

RICHARD

It was fun. The other writers on the show were a lot of fun and they taught me a lot. The producer was a little bit odd because he had originally conceived this show for a vehicle starring Groucho Marx. So it was a little bit of a stretch. I lasted two years on there and then television started to come in. They cut the budget on the show and I was let go and I had to look around for other things. I managed to find quite a few jobs in radio. They didn't pay very much but they were enough to keep me going. I got so I was writing maybe a show a week. It was a lot of work. I did a syndicated show starring Fred MacMurray and Irene Dunne, did twenty-six weeks on that.

STAN

These were original shows? That's an awful lot of work, all that dialogue, to do in a week.

RICHARD

I didn't know any different then.

STAN

What did you refer to? As a writer, you need a reference of some kind. You wouldn't even have time to research these stories.

RICHARD

It was comedy so you didn't really have to research them. I made them up. I remembered my old short stories.

STAN

The short stories you read as a kid?

RICHARD

Very roughly, very roughly.

STAN

So you were primarily a long-form writer in those days, as compared to a joke writer, you were a serious writer.

RICHARD

Generally I work by myself. So I had no choice, I had to write everything.

STAN

You continued to write radio. Then you went into television. When did you write *Topper*?

RICHARD

I wrote *Topper*, it must have been in the middle '50s. But just to go back for one minute to radio, as I told you, I was very disappointed in Edgar Bergen's response. But then I became acquainted with some writers for his show and it made me a little happier that I didn't end up on his show. Because Edgar Bergen had a flight instructor—he was taking flying lessons—and the instructor's name was Zeno Clinker and Zeno fancied himself as a joke writer and he convinced Bergen that he was a joke writer. What Zeno would do, he would lie in bed and dictate all his thoughts. They came out as one-liners. Then he would send the tape to Bergen, who would have them transcribed and there'd be about a page-and-a-half of one-line jokes. And then when the writers came in with a story for the week, Bergen would hand them this page-and-a-half of what the writers called "Zeno's clinkers" and tell them to work them in. It was a very tough job. One more thing about radio: most of the stuff I did was syndicated in radio so I didn't get paid too much, but I got a chance to do a show for the other Dick Powell, on *Richard Diamond, Private Eye*, which paid me I think seven hundred dollars, and it was about a ventriloquist who comes to see Richard Diamond and says he wants Richard Diamond to kill this associate of his, whom he hates because the associate gets all the laughs, gets all the girls, is the bright one, the witty one, and he can't stand him and wants him killed. And, of course, it turns out that he's talking about his dummy. So the other Dick Powell happened to be a good friend of Edgar Bergen's, so naturally he got Edgar Bergen to play the part on the radio show. When it came time to do it, in a studio with no audience, Bergen came in, then his helper came in carrying a box which turned out to contain Charlie, his dummy. And the helper asked where he should put Charlie for the show. And Dick Powell kind of did a double take but suggested a location, all of which made me realize that what I'd written as a fantasy had quite a bit of reality to it. But going from there, a couple of days later there was a meeting in Hollywood, an anti-blacklisting meeting which had to do with a publication, published in New York, called *Red Channels*, which was a book about two inches thick which contained the name of every actor, writer, or producer who had ever gone on a march, gone to a meeting. It was, in effect, an attempt to get these people blacklisted and it was very effective. The people who put it out were talking about putting out a Hollywood edition, so there was a mass meeting against it and I was one of the speakers. Several days after that, I came to the producer of *The Richard Diamond Show* and said, "Since everybody liked the show, I guess I'm going to do a lot more." And she said that she was sorry to tell me that since my name had been in the "trades" as being a speaker at that meeting, the agency had put me on the blacklist. From there on, it was kind of a creeping blacklist. I could work in some places, not in others. Even going into television, I could work under my own name quite often, though sometimes not. I did early television programs like Joan Davis. Then I was involved in union politics in the Writers Guild and the Radio Writers Guild, of which I was a member at that time, was involved in a television jurisdiction battle with the Screen Writers Guild and a lot of red-baiting went on, unfortunately, and that didn't help me out at all. Gradually I found myself almost completely blacklisted.

STAN
For speaking your mind.

RICHARD
Yes. When I went to work on *Topper*, I worked under the name of the head writer on the show, who understood my situation and was willing to put his name on it. Of course, the only

difficulty with it was that I was getting half-scale but what could I do?

STAN

That blacklist period was such an unfortunate time for writers and I think it's important for people to understand that simply because you expressed your opinions, you were cut off from your life's work.

RICHARD

This was the time of the Hollywood Ten and everybody in Hollywood was scared to death. It was really a time of panic.

STAN

And yet you stood your ground.

RICHARD

More or less, as much as I could.

STAN

But you paid a price for it. That's part of the history of Hollywood.

RICHARD

I wasn't really as bad off as the actors, because I could work as a writer. Actors couldn't hide their faces. They sold shoes.

STAN

I want to ask you about what we're seeing in the media these days, a kind of lack of culture or the wrong message going out on the medium, that writers really have no control of their product. Or am I wrong about that? Do writers have control? Do they have responsibility, in your eyes, for what they write for television? How can you turn down a buck?

RICHARD

It's a many-pronged question. I think everybody is basically responsible for what he or she writes but there's the

85

reality of eating. And if you write something that you know is not going to be accepted, then you better turn it into a play or a book, if you can. Because the avenues are just not open anymore. Let's talk a little bit about the Golden Age of Television. I wasn't really part of that because that was happening in New York, where they had all the anthology shows, had a different show every week. And they relied mainly on playwrights, writers for Broadway, who were accustomed and had a lot of stuff in their trunks. And they were writing things that were topical, had some content. It was the Golden Age. They also had great comedy shows, like *Your Show of Shows* with Sid Caesar. But gradually a couple of things happened. One was that the people who controlled television got nervous about the content of some of these shows and they couldn't control it. It used to be that a writer would come in and give the producer something he had worked on and loved and if the producer loved it, he would put it on the air and that was it. Strange things could happen in the middle of a show. Somebody gets shot who shouldn't have gotten shot, but once cameras started rolling, that was it.

Well, the powers that be got terribly nervous about this and their answer was to move it all to Hollywood and put it on film and also to do away with the anthology shows and make them more star vehicles, which they did. And that narrowed the opportunities for really saying anything on television. I always tried to give my work a certain reality but the area was very circumscribed, really. And as far as violence on television, that goes way back. It was in the '60s, after the assassinations of Bobby Kennedy and Martin Luther King, there was a lot of talk generally about whether the violence on television was responsible or was it merely reflecting what was happening. And the Senate Subcommittee on Communications had a hearing on violence. I was selected from the Writers Guild to go and be a spokesman for the Writers Guild. And what I tried to tell them was this: that violence in itself has always been a part of art but it hasn't been unmotivated violence. That is, if violence is going to be shown, the reason for it should be shown. What kind of character is committing the violence, why, the impact on the bereaved after the people were shot or killed by whatever means, and it should be shown for what it really is instead of being just a device to hook in the audience. I didn't get very far.

STAN

I recall that a number of years ago, when I had my first experience writing a Western, working with a collaborator. I said to my partner, "Three people just got shot in the bar. What do we do?: And he said, "Pan away." And it seems that's how it's done in these movies today, with the violence, it's cut away, pan away, and nobody has any identity. I feel, as you do, that it kind of makes people insensitive. Or am I a bleeding heart?

RICHARD

Well, you may be a bleeding heart but that's beside the point. I think it's the lack of dealing with reality, dramatic reality, what our situation really is today, what really are the problems the people face, the country faces. And that is apparently taboo. And violence inevitably creeps in to fill in the void. If you can't talk about reality, then you go to violence. And I think they have narrowed the audience down to a youth segment, a youth-oriented audience, and alienated the people who would want to go and see real stories about real people. I'm not very optimistic about the situation because you can't give advice to a young writer to write what you feel and then submit it for a movie, because you know it's not going to sell. You can tell them to write what they feel and put it in a book or put it in a play, but that's not a very big field, especially plays these days.

STAN

I think what you're saying is right on, Richard. The writer in television these days is kind of a prisoner to the whole system.

RICHARD

Television and, I think, motion pictures, unfortunately. The film schools are turning out hundreds or thousands of new writers every year. The competition is tremendous, and what they're buying are violent scripts, so not much else is being written that I know of.

STAN

But there's obviously room for the personal story, the character-motivated story, as opposed to the plot-motivated story.

RICHARD

There's room for that, but is it salable? That's the other question. My movie going, my wife and I probably see maybe three or four foreign movies to every domestic movie, which is kind of a sad thing. I wish it weren't true but that's just the way I feel these days.

STAN

I did see a nice picture featuring Jessica Tandy, called *Camilla*, that was a character-motivated film. Mostly it's been foreign films that were character-motivated. *Forrest Gump* actually was a character-motivated film, which I felt was a very interesting and compelling movie. But the overall view I see is that it's still guns and glory kind of stuff.

RICHARD

You and I were talking about the Paul Newman picture, *Nobody's Fool*, which I thought was a very good picture but that was made from a book, the screenplay was from a book. And if that had just been written as a movie, would it have been sold? I don't know. I would hope so but I don't know.

STAN

You know, Richard, our time is leaving us now.

RICHARD

I shouldn't have been so fascinating. It went too fast.

STAN

You are, indeed, a fascinating person. What are you working on now, anything specific?

RICHARD

Like everybody else, I write spec screenplays which don't get sold. And I also write angry letters to the editor about the outrage of the day. And that's about it.

STAN

Do you find that ageism is prevalent today in Hollywood for writers?

RICHARD

I'm sure it is. Say I had a dynamite idea for a series on television. I would be walking in to pitch it to a room full of people from their early twenties to their late twenties. And they would be staring at me. There would be no rapport.

STAN

And that basically is what is happening with older writers these days. I've heard the same thing from other writers. They're better off having their son or daughter go in there to do the pitch.

RICHARD

I've got a son. I'm training him.

STAN

Richard, our time has vanished, gone, kaput. I could listen to you for hours because your wisdom is decidedly right on.

RICHARD

To use a cliché, you're too kind.

STAN

So we're closing the show and I want to thank Richard Powell, writer/producer, who has shared with us some of his experiences. Thank you very much, Richard.

Joan Scott

Norma Barzman

Chapter Four

Today's Guests

NORMA BARZMAN
Screenwriter and Novelist

and

JOAN SCOTT
Screen and Television Writer

OCTOBER 1997

STAN

Hi, ladies and gentlemen, and welcome to *The Stanley Dyrector Show*. We are privileged today to have as our guests the uniquely multi-talented ladies: Norma Barzman and Joan Scott. Norma has written for the screen and television, newspapers, books. A few of her many credits are the film *Never Say Goodbye*, a comedy with Errol Flynn. Did you know that? She also wrote *The Locket* and *Young Man with Ideas* and some collaborations with her late husband Ben Barzman, the renowned screenwriter who was a victim of the infamous blacklist. And Norma was blacklisted too, I might say.

Joan Scott has written for many television shows: *Marcus Welby*, *The Waltons*. She worked on projects with Walt Disney, was a consultant on the Robert De Niro film about the Blacklist called *Guilty by Suspicion*. Joan is now in the midst of completing her book about her life with her late husband, writer-producer Adrian Scott, who was one of the Hollywood Ten. Adrian was sent to prison because of that witch hunt. Joan's book is called *Adrian's Wife*. Norma, in the book *Tender Comrades*, I read where you said something to the effect that your life was kind of like a screwball comedy in Hollywood.

NORMA

Well, what I meant was that after, not fleeing but leaving the United States in sort of a hurry and going to England to do a film—and I left everything in the bureau drawers at 1290 Sunset Plaza Drive and thought we would be back in six weeks—we left for six weeks and stayed thirty years. And so I think that, in itself, is pretty funny. I never got any of the belongings back, but, well, I guess what's funny, or what's marvelous, is the contrast. I feel sorry about it because the other blacklistees will say that it was a terrible time and they are right. Careers were broken, lives were lost. The children, the effect on the children was terrible and we felt guilty, because in France, where we went, we had a charmed life, and that's part of what I meant. We had a house that was more Hollywood than any Hollywood house we had had, with a swimming pool and tennis court and out in the country and around the corner from where Picasso lived. So it was a marvelous life.

STAN

Well, Joan, I understand that you were Adrian Scott's front also, you were your husband's front. Can you tell us a little bit about that?

JOAN

Yes. Well, he of course couldn't appear at studios for conferences. He'd be recognized. And he could write under the table, doing somebody's script or fixing a play. But when it came down to making an appearance for a television show, to go in and confer with the producers and so forth, he couldn't do that.

STAN

Here was a man who wrote *Murder My Sweet,* which was kind of like a tough-guy, private-eye yarn, as I recall, with Dick Powell. I mean, he wrote those kind of characters. How could you handle questions about such things?

JOAN

When I went in as his front, it was a period when we wore fluffy skirts and petticoats under them. What was that, 1950? I was fronting for him from about the mid-50s.

NORMA

It must have been in the '50s, yes, after we were gone.

JOAN

And there weren't many women; I don't know if there were. There was one other woman television writer at that time, and so I was kind of an oddity. And then when I'd come in looking puffy, they'd say, "This is a girl who writes like a man" and everybody would come in to see this. And poor Adrian had to do rewrites on the scripts and we'd have some tiffs over that. But mostly it was just dreary and depressing for him.

STAN

I'm sure it was.

JOAN

We didn't have a charmed life. We were living in a little tract house in Van Nuys and we made part of the garage into his office. And they were lean and difficult times for most of that time.

STAN

Norma, let me ask you this - how did you manage?

NORMA

Well, our experience was so different from Joan's and Adrian's. We went over to France after making the film in England, never really expecting to stay but actually it was Adrian who encouraged us to stay. We went to England to help break the blacklist, to see to it that Eddie Dmytryk, who couldn't work anymore in America, could maybe direct a film in England—*Christ in Concrete*—and it was a beautiful film and he did direct it, but as we all know, after he directed it he wound up naming names before HUAC. Ben had given up a job at MGM. I had two babies and one in the tummy and a sick mother and was in the middle of my analysis, my psychoanalysis. It was no time for me to go. But we gave up a charmed life in Hollywood to go and break the Blacklist for Eddie, who said, "You've got to give me this chance to work. It's the only way." And Ben wrote the screenplay nights and weekends and then Eddie called us and said. "Yes, Rank does want to do it." And so we left, just like that.

STAN

Before we continue, I would like to get your comments about some of the photographs you brought with you that we've been talking about. What memories do they invoke?

NORMA

There's a very beautiful shot of Joan and Adrian and Mike, the war orphan Adrian adopted when he was in England. And another, of six of my seven children, walking up to the entrance way to our Mougins house, where we lived the charmed life.

STAN

That's in France, right?

NORMA

In France, in the south of France. Our seventh child wasn't born yet. We lived very near Picasso. And there's a shot of Adrian and me and we had funny expressions on our faces because Adrian had just said to me, "Norma, I'm going to go back and face the music; if need be, go to jail. I don't think they'll ever do that. I've been sentenced, I've been cited for contempt but I don't think they'll ever sentence me to jail, but I've gotta go back." And he said, "You, Norma, stay in France; you and Ben."

STAN

And there is one photo that seems to be of a painting.

NORMA

That's a wonderful portrait of him by the artist, Joe Hirsch, who was likewise blacklisted. Nobody thinks of artists being blacklisted, but he had a very hard time in America and sailed to France with his family. And he's a great painter who hangs in the Museum of Modern Art.

STAN

And there's one photo that seems to include Ingrid Bergman in the middle of the group.

NORMA

No, that's me when I was young, during the shooting of *El Cid* and it's Ben, my husband, on my left and the director of *El Cid*, Anthony Mann, on my right. And, of course, Ben still doesn't have, even after all Paul Jarrico's struggling to get Ben's name on the film, still doesn't have his name on it, because Phil Yordan, who was the front, and who only, even in his own words, only did the business stuff and never wrote a word for it, will not give Ben, still will not give Ben credit on *El Cid*, which is a magnificent film.

STAN

Tell me about the book, *Tender Comrades.*

NORMA

That book tells all these stories. It's a wonderful new book that's going to be published on November 12th and that has an interview with Joan, and an interview with me, and an interview with many of our friends, like Jules Dassin, the director who did one picture with Ben, and so forth.

STAN

You're in the opening of the book and Joan is on page 585, I know that.

NORMA

Joan is on page 585.

JOAN

The author is Pat McGilligan.

NORMA

And Paul Buhle.

JOAN

And Paul Buhle.

NORMA

And it's a wonderful book. And Joan is in there, and I'm the first interview there, and we tell a lot about what went on during the blacklist period.

STAN

You know, Joan, I read in the book that you worked with Walt Disney. Can you tell us something about Walt Disney? Because there's a little story I read, and you can tell us a great deal about it, when one of Walt Disney's aides came up to you and asked you what you were. Can you tell us what that was about?

JOAN

Before I was married, I had a rather distinctive name, LaCour, Joan LaCour, and so people automatically assumed it was French and there was no question about what other elements there might be. But as Joanne Court, you know, people would say, "What is that?" And I hadn't prepared for that, my ethnic background. So at one point, on the stairs from Walt's office, his top aide came down and said, "Well, we need to know what you are." And I said, "What do you mean?" He said, "Well, you know, Scottish, French, whatever." And I said, cause I knew that Walt was anti-semitic (and, among other things, anti-trade unions), "Well, I'm mostly French but I'm this and that," and I said, "and I'm one-eighth Jewish." Couldn't resist it. But working with him was pretty intimidating, you know. You know, he wanted to be called Uncle Walt, but people froze against the wall.

STAN

But you worked on *Beethoven* with him. Was that a film or a documentary?

JOAN

It started out with leftover *Fantasia* footage, with Mickey Mouse, and he asked for some research on it. I guess he didn't know about Beethoven. And when he saw it, he said, "Oh, this is an hour television at least." Well, it ended up being two hours and it was released in Europe as a feature film.

NORMA

I think it's awfully important for people to understand that there were many women screenwriters at the time, many who were blacklisted, like Joan and me. One of the others was Marguerite Roberts, who had been at Metro for many years and had one of the top salaries in Hollywood, and she was called in to Louis B. Mayer and told, just in one minute, "We're going to take your name off of' *Ivanhoe.* Sign this, saying that you're willing for us to do that and we're just gonna give you your money for that and then we want you to just get off the lot immediately." And she never worked again. And there were many who were not yet as successful as Maggie Roberts, like Bess Taffel, many, many others, and for them, it was much harder than for the men, because it was really the beginnings of their career, just as it was for mine. I only had a few credits and when I went off to Europe, nobody had ever heard of me. They had heard of Ben. He had many credits and then he kept on writing and had more than thirty-five credits, even without the pictures that he didn't have his name on. But my experience was that it was hard to get a job and my passport was lifted. I couldn't travel. I finally had a film shooting in Italy but couldn't go to it while it was shooting, because I had no passport. That was *Luxury Girls*, a United Artists release. The man who directed it was Bernard Vorhaus and they put an Italian's name on even as the Director, because Bernard Vorhaus had been named. They put an Italian man's name on as being the author of the screenplay, although I had written the whole screenplay alone. It was made at Cinecitta in 1953. It was a beautiful little film and I think it went to the Edinburgh Festival, but we haven't been able to get a copy of it. Because if we do, we can get it to the San Francisco Festival in the spring. And they're putting my name back on it as sole screenplay author.

STAN

You ladies have really gone through the mill, I might say, of Hollywood. You have really suffered the hard times that others probably can only read about. And in reading *Tender Comrades*, I recall reading a little piece where Joan was advised by Adrian Scott not to give in to all of Walt Disney's demands. Can you tell us a little bit about that, Joan?

JOAN

Well, at one point, Disney had me sitting right next to him and in a circle were all the yes-men, the musicians, producers. And it was hard for me to make eye contact with this man, he had such an aura. And one minute, he'd be very sweet and the next minute, he'd be pounding books and scripts on the floor. So these were men who, I don't think there was a woman there at the time, in production, but these people had been there like twenty years. And one of them, when the *Beethoven* film was shot in Vienna, said one thing about a location shot and he was fired on the spot by Disney. And also another funny thing was, when I was reading some of my ideas for *Beethoven*, who went deaf at a very convenient point in his life, about halfway through, so you could divide the shows up, and I was allowed to put in my ideas, I worked with the composer and anything you write over the Ninth sounds very important, very meaningful. But my husband had warned me that when I first saw it I would hate it, that they'd have changed everything and they'd have added things I didn't like and he said, "Walt's probably going to be sitting behind you in the projection room and when the lights go on, you're going to have to have something to say." So the next day, that happened and Walt touched me on the shoulder and he said, "Well, how'd you like it?" And I said, "Walt, you've done it again." That was Adrian's line.

STAN

And so very diplomatic.

NORMA

It's funny, they both had that line. Maybe Ben remembered from Adrian. He used to do that at the end of a projection of the film when he didn't know what to say to the producer, or he didn't know what to say to the director, he'd say that too, "You've done it again." I think he must have gotten it from Adrian.

STAN

Norma, in the book I also read that a blond-headed lady tipped you off that they were after you to serve a subpoena or something. Tell us what happened.

NORMA

You know what it was a very, very, very hot day and we did something which we never did before and never did after, we were sitting out on the front lawn on Sunset Plaza Drive. We were trying to get a breeze, if there was one, and a car came up and into our driveway, with this lovely, tousled blond, so beautiful, we didn't know who she was, driving. She said, "I want to warn you that at the bottom of your hill, the Sheriff's car is there and there are two men in the Sheriff's car and they stop people to find out what number Sunset Plaza Drive they're going to. I'm on my way to Judy Garland's party, which is further up the hill than you, but they really want to see who is going here, as if something is happening here, a meeting or something. I think you should know." And we didn't know who she was. She said, "My name's Norma." And I said, "Well, my name's Norma." And she said, "Well, I think we're gonna change it." And we didn't know who she was until we were reading the *Paris Herald* at a cafe and there was Marilyn Monroe.

STAN

Also known as Norma Jean Baker.

NORMA

Right ,that's who that was, warning us that we were being watched. But we didn't have much of that stuff, the being watched and the being trailed and the being frightened. The only thing, I think I mentioned, was that in France, when you didn't have papers, you didn't have a passport, you felt you might have to leave the country right away. And so we did feel hunted for a while. But after that first scariness of it, we began to meet the great intellectuals. I had mentioned Picasso before, but we also met their great poet, Paul Eluard; their great scientists, Monsieur Joliot-Curie and Irene Curie. And we were so welcomed. And I think the important thing, why we had such a charmed life, was because France felt we were heroes. We had come there. We had stood up to the Committee. We weren't going to give names for them. Our doctors in France wouldn't let us pay for services. We were really welcomed in a way. Well, the best thing is that shortly before my husband died, he received the Order of Arts and Letters from the French Ministry of Culture. And they really felt that we had become part of their cultural life and it was a great life.

STAN

Joan, in the book *Tender Comrades*, you allude to the fact that Hollywood really killed Adrian Scott.

JOAN

Well, the Hollywood Blacklist certainly did, because at the tender age of 34, usually in those days, producers were old, gray-haired or bald, and cigar-smoking. And for someone at 34 to become a producer was unheard of. And when he made his film *Crossfire*, which was nominated for an Academy Award that year. . .

STAN

That was the first film about anti-semitism, am I correct?

JOAN

Yes, yes.

STAN

That was before *Gentlemen's Agreement*?

JOAN

Yes, the first one, and it was well received and soon was financially successful. He had done other films but that was the one he liked to be known for.

STAN

It was a great part for Robert Ryan.

JOAN

Yes. And that was the crossfire idea , that somebody gets caught in the crossfire of bullets, as he did in the end. They were having trouble finding a name for it. And in the end, Robert Ryan is running off and he's caught between the detective and somebody else firing at him. So it became *Crossfire*.

STAN

Norma, what about Paul Jarrico?

NORMA

Well, that's just what I was going to say to you, that in this book, Paul's interview is wonderful. And Paul just died last Tuesday and we're trying to get over it. But he died so triumphantly. It's so extraordinary. I've never come across a story like that, because he had a goal: he was going to get credits for blacklisted writers, he was going to see to it that the Guild concentrated on getting those credits for them.

STAN

The Writers Guild of America/West.

NORMA

The Writers Guild of America/West, yes. And he also was going to try to see to it, and he did so wonderfully that the Guilds of Hollywood would admit that they had pursued a terrible, terrible thing when they agreed to let the Blacklist stay and for so long. And it's only a week ago Monday night that there was a huge ceremony at the Academy, where the presidents, the four presidents of the Screen Actors Guild, the Screen Directors Guild, the Screen Writers Guild and AFTRA (the television actors) had apologized, but officially, to the blacklisted people and said this must never happen again. Really what was important was that it was recognized that it was against the First Amendment to look into peoples' beliefs. And this was wonderfully done and Paul was, well, he was the soul of this fight and when he got killed the next day, after another event honoring blacklistees, just on his way home, so weary from having led the good fight that he lost control of the car, fell asleep and was instantly killed when his car went into a tree. So that we really felt terrible, but this story was magnificent in the sense that someone, right up to the end, pursued his goal and saw it through and triumphed. And, I'll tell you what happened with me was that Monday night, there had been the wonderful evening at the Academy and there was no coverage in the *Los Angeles Times* on Tuesday and there was no coverage in the *Los Angeles Times* on Wednesday. And someone from the Guild called me and said, "Norma, can you do anything? Cause you're an old newspaper woman, you're an old LA newspaper woman." Which I was; I'd been a reporter on the old *Los Angeles Examiner* in the 40s, when the war was on. So I called the managing editor of the *Los Angeles Times,* who had been my editor over at the *Herald-Examiner,* and I told him that I thought this was one of the great feature stories. If I'd had a story like this when I was young, I would've been delirious because I felt so terrible about Paul's death. But the truth was that it had within it, the struggle, the sadness and the triumph that we really have all experienced. And he said, "Okay." First he argued with me and said, "Well, we covered all that in Calendar, and really that's enough." And I said, "No, you've covered the 50th anniversary of the Blacklist, but this is what's important, that we really won, on Monday night, for all the Guilds to apologize and really the producers too ,because it was with their assent, and that was the big moment and that was what we had been fighting for and it was a great victory for Paul." And finally, the managing editor said, "All right, I will do it. I can't promise the first page, but I will see to it personally." And he did.

102

And the next day, it appeared on the first page and he called me and said, "Norma, you were right. It was important and I'm glad you did." And for me, it was like the peak of my newspaper career.

STAN

You know, Joan, in reading *Tender Comrades*, I get this melancholy feeling about your feelings about losing Adrian. And it really comes through in the story that is related in this book. What a great loss it was. Can you give us a couple of words?

JOAN

Adrian couldn't ever be employed here again and we went to England in '61, where he could work. And then, our stay there of seven years was interrupted by an offer from Universal Studios for Adrian to come back under a two-year contract. Why they did this, I don't know, because they didn't attempt to use the qualities he had brought with him to the industry: you know, humane values and humanist concepts. And they just sort of let him sit around there, doing nothing. And it was, you know, they bought up his contract and he couldn't write. He was so depressed. This was one more light at the end of the tunnel that had gone out. And I think he felt he had nowhere left to turn.

STAN

Do you know that our time has almost run out? And I wanted to get maybe ten seconds of what are you guys doing now.

JOAN

Well, I'm writing a book about my life with Adrian, called *Adrian's Wife*, and I can go either for a movie or a book. If I can interest Annette Bening and Warren Beatty, that would be nice. I worked with Annette and my husband worked with Warren Beatty in London and I think they'd be great for it.

STAN

That would be great. And Norma?

NORMA

Well, I've just finished a second novel, *The Violins of Cremona*, which I hope to get published soon. There's no use going into what it's about, four days in Cremona, realizing that the idol of your life is not what he seemed. What I'm now doing is starting a novel, that does take place in Paris in the '50s and '60s and has a lot about the Blacklist period.

STAN

Well, we're gonna continue talking with our guests while the show is going off the air. I want to thank my beautiful guests, Norma Barzman and Joan Scott. This is a memorial, this show, to Paul Jarrico and also, by the way, to Adrian Scott and to Ben Barzman. Thank you.

This show is dedicated to the memory of screenwriter
Paul Jarrico 1915 – 1997

Chapter Five

THE STANLEY DYRECTOR SHOW

Today's Guests

NORMA BARZMAN

and

ROBERT WHITE
Screenwriters/Authors

2003

STAN

Hello, ladies and gentlemen, and welcome once again to *The Stanley Dyrector Show*. We have one heck of a show for you today. We have two guests who are screenwriters and authors. Robert White has been a guest on this show before with his wife, Phyllis White, who has since passed away. On this show, we're going to talk about a number of things Robert has written, as well as how he puts a piece of work together. Norma Barzman has also been a visitor on our show before, when we talked about the Blacklist. Actually, we've talked about the Blacklist a number of times, with Bob and Phyllis and with Norma and Joan Scott as well. Norma is also going to tell us how to put a novel together.

First, let me talk to Robert. I know that you lost Phyllis recently and she co-authored with you the book, *Hollywood & The Best of Los Angeles Alive!*

Robert White

Norma Barzman, Robert White, Stan

ROBERT

You want to know about the book. I think people are interested, usually, in how things come about. Phyllis and I were screenwriters here in town for many years. Every time a friend or relative would come here from somewhere else, it was always "Can you introduce us to stars? Can you show us in the studios how movies are made?" Two years ago, the Los Angeles Visitors Bureau did a survey of visitors and asked, "What are the most important things you want to see and do when you're in Los Angeles?" Over eighty percent said they wanted to see stars and wanted to see movies being made. So we thought there isn't any book like that and that's the book we should write. First we did a couple years of research while we were doing other projects. Once we signed a contract with Hunter Publishing, we spent a year doing more research while we were writing the book. We ended up with six hundred pages and an immense number of facts, a survey of Hollywood, the relationship of Hollywood organically, the whole area of the movies, and the relationship between the movie industry and the people who live here. It gives the history, the background, and a lot of stories.

STAN

We'll hear more about those stories a little later. Norma, you used to write with your husband, Ben Barzman.

NORMA

Yes, I did. I even wrote a novel with him, which I brought today, that we wrote together twenty years ago, *Rich Dreams*. That was not our title, that was a computerized title that Warner Books, after buying it from us for $200,000, wanted to make it into a paperback. I got an extra $50,000 from them for doing it in paperback and it was never hardcover. It came out twenty years ago and was a satire on the Harold Robbins kind of book, which was then very, very popular. It was my idea to do a book that satirized what was the popular book novel of the time, just the way Jane Austen did in *Northanger Abbey*, her first book, which satirized the gothic novel, which was very popular in her time. Then she went on to do the Jane Austen kind of novel that we all love, like *Pride and Prejudice.*

STAN

I read *Rich Dreams* a number of years ago. I believe you made a lot of money on this book. Tell us how much.

NORMA

A quarter of a million dollars. Warner Books paid us a quarter of a million and yet we had no success with it in the United States, but when it went to France, they knew it was satire, they loved it, we got great reviews in *Le Monde* and *Figaro Littéraire*, and it went into paperback and book club and it was all over France and it made a big success, which shows you that a book can succeed. Even though they paid so much for it here, they didn't get anything back because they didn't push it and it didn't work, nobody knew what it was. It was sold as if it were a romance novel, which it isn't. It was sold in a horrible way, with a little window peeking at two lovers, on the cover.

STAN

There was a reason, Norma, why you got out of this country. Clue us in about that.

NORMA

We were blacklisted and we left here before the subpoenas got to us. We left here, really running to make a film in England, *Christ in Concrete*, which is going to come out soon on DVD. Americans haven't seen it, but it's a really great film. So we went there to make a film. We thought we would do the film and go over to France for a vacation and probably come back. We left all our belongings at 1290 Sunset Plaza Drive, our house here, and we stayed in France for thirty years—not six or eight weeks, but thirty years. We left Hollywood in February 1949 and we came back in 1979, thirty years later.

STAN

I must share with our audience a wonderful piece of trivia. You and Ben were tipped off that the FBI was coming by a very big superstar. Tell us how that happened.

NORMA

By Marilyn Monroe. That's a wonderful story. We were just sitting on the front lawn, which we never did, but it was one of those Santa Ana terribly hot days, and a car whizzed up our hill and stopped at our house, came into the driveway and a beautiful blond came out of the car and said, "Do you guys know that at the bottom of your hill there's a Sheriff's car and they're stopping every car going up the hill to see where they're going, whether they're going to come to your house, 1290?" We asked how that could be and she asked whether we were going to have a meeting or something. We were, in fact, planning a meeting of the First Amendment Committee because the Hollywood Ten were already in Washington and a lot of stars were going to come to our house and plan a protest of the HUAC hearings. We would have gotten our subpoenas if we'd stuck around, but we didn't. We left in time.

STAN

Bob, I know that you were blacklisted too.

ROBERT

It was a completely different situation with Norma and the hard-core blacklistees. They were among no one knows how many, there were hundreds, several hundred at least, writers and actors who were also blacklisted; they had to leave the country, they had to work with a "front," under a different name, that kind of situation. I'm an illustration of what happened beyond the obvious stupidity of the blacklist. It went on to sheer ignorance and affected even more people, perhaps into the thousands, if you count the people who were not the Communist Party people who were blacklisted, but the people who were graylisted and the people who were swept up into the maw of this machinery that knew not what it was doing. For instance, I was working at Screen Gems, the Columbia television subsidary at the time. This was the early 1950s, 1952 or something like that. I'd been working there steadily for a couple of years, going from one show to another, writing some pilots, and suddenly I was out, my office was cleaned out, I was out the door and I couldn't get any work there anymore, and nobody would say why.

Finally, my agent discovered that I'd been blacklisted. And I said, "Moi?" And he couldn't find out why I was blacklisted, because everyone insisted there was no such thing as a blacklist, it would be illegal, they didn't have a blacklist. Eventually he found a friend who worked at the studio who said he would look at the blacklist, and he came back and reported that Robert P. White was blacklisted because he signed something when he was in college in Michigan. To which I said, "I'm Robert A. White and I was never in college in Michigan," and that was the end of my blacklisting. Can you imagine how many people were on a list like that? Every studio had its own list. It wasn't like there was an official, industry-wide, blacklist. If there were twenty studios, there were twenty lists, and the television networks had other lists, and the producers had people whispering in their ears.

It was bad enough that the blacklist was focused on folks who were trying to exercise their First Amendment rights, but in addition, with no logic involved, at all, it just swept up everyone in sight, including besides those in Hollywood, teachers, doctors, labor organizers, electricians, anybody who'd ever signed anything.

STAN
Really. I didn't know about teachers being blacklisted.

NORMA
Teachers and professors at universities were let go.

ROBERT
The University of California at Berkeley was just decimated by the blacklist, because there were a lot of progressives there, a lot of people who refused to sign any kind of loyalty oath.

NORMA

It was a terrible period. And it's very similar to the period that we are now in. It is so similar because the Cold War was used as an excuse to take away our civil liberties, just as the "War Against Terror" is getting to be an excuse to take away our liberties. Anyway, I think it's very important for people to know about the blacklist, which is why I wrote a memoir, *The Red and the Blacklist*, which is coming out in April 2003. The subtitle is *The Intimate Memoir of a Hollywood Expatriate*. And I was an expatriate and so was my husband. We were both screenwriters who left here thinking we were leaving for six to eight weeks, and stayed thirty years in France, had a house in Paris, bought a house in the South of France, near Picasso's house, knew Picasso. We had a really great life for thirty years in Europe and made wonderful films. *El Cid* was one of them, made in Spain under Bronston, and my husband only got posthumous credit on *El Cid* in 1999, during the furor over Kazan getting an Oscar. I got my "written by" credit on an original screenplay I had done, which was shot in Italy, at Cinecittá.

STAN

You had a front, didn't you?

NORMA

Yes, Ennio Flaiano, they put on an Italian writer's name—that's off now—and they also put on an Italian director's name because it was directed by an American blacklisted director, Bernard Vorhaus. They took off his name and put on another Italian's name.

STAN

What was the English title of that movie?

NORMA

Luxury Girls. It was a tender study of adolescents. United Artists, which was the distributor, booked it into an all-night movie theater on 42nd Street and put nude girlie photos outside as if they were in the picture, which they weren't, and they gave it the title *Luxury Girls* instead of my title, *Finishing School.*

ROBERT

I was thinking as Norma described being forced, as a writer to go to France, but then spends thirty wonderful years in Paris and the South of France, about a writer's life, even those who aren't paid a quarter of a million advance for a book. I've got to tell people, the country is full of people who would like to be writers and realize the poverty that comes with it most of the time. But with Phyllis and me, we were both writers individually, and then we got married and then collaborated all the years we were married. During that time we never made a real fortune; it never went up in the millions, but we worked at home at our own pace. When we lived in the Valley we had a pool, then we moved out to the beach. We hardly ever had to go the studio, except to talk about a story. We always resisted having an office in the studio when possible.

STAN

When you were writing *My Favorite Martian*?

ROBERT

Yes, all of those things, all of those sit-coms. *My Favorite Martian* was the one on which we got stuck and had to be in the studio. We had a really wonderful life, because we were doing something that we really enjoyed doing. And I know so many people, mostly non-writers, who spend their entire lives going to an office and doing something that they don't like and sometimes that they hate. Life can be very different in the case of writers, especially writers working in Hollywood, because writers working in Hollywood are members of the Writers Guild, and as members of the Writers Guild, you have a pension, you have healthcare, a wonderful health plan.

NORMA

And we have all those things because we went out on strike and we struggled for it. Young writers forget that.

ROBERT

If you're a novelist or someone like that, you don't have that fallback position. But a writer working in Hollywood kind of has the best of all worlds. You're doing something that you'd do if nobody paid you, that you love to do.

NORMA

I had an experience similar to Bob. That is, I was a writer and Ben was a writer. I was the first girl reporter on the *Los Angeles Examiner* and while I was there, I wrote a story, *Never Say Goodbye*, which Warner Brothers bought for Errol Flynn. So it goes way back, and my husband was a screenwriter and we did have the charmed life. I do want to amend that somewhat. Yes, we had a marvelous thirty years and a really great life abroad, but the people who were blacklisted and stayed in this country suffered so much and it has to be made clear how much they suffered. Adrian Scott, who was a Christ-like character, a wonderful person who was one of the Hollywood Ten, his health was ruined. Several blacklisted people killed themselves, they couldn't work anymore. Their marriages were broken up and their children suffered a great deal. So the blacklist usually destroyed and we were just lucky.

ROBERT

We don't want to give the impression that it was a jolly time and everybody had a lot of fun.

NORMA

We are the lucky few. We had a great, great life and we're still having one, because we're writing.

STAN

Robert, tell us more about your book.

ROBERT

This is the book that Phyllis and I wrote last year. We got the manuscript in and then she died before it was published, so she never saw it. I just want to tell you what makes us qualified to write a book like this about Hollywood. In the December 26

113

issue of *TV Guide*, the lead story is called "Tribute 2002," which was about thirty-nine people who died in that year who had the greatest effect on the arts and entertainment, like Milton Berle, Billy Wilder, a bunch of giants. Here's what they said about Phyllis:

"Was there a more eclectic TV scribe? In the '50s, White was head writer for the *Tonight Show*, won a Peabody for penning the documentary series *Adventure*. Later she wrote Westerns (*The Virginian*), crime shows (*Mission Impossible*), sit-coms (*The Flying Nun*) and soaps (*The Guiding Light*). White died at 79."

It was a hell of a career. As for the book itself, let me read a couple of excerpts just to give you an idea of what it's like. Tippi Hedren wrote a long preface for us and at the end of it she says,

"This book is fun. It reads especially well with a tub of buttery popcorn and a box of Good n' Plenty. I read with interest that there are over sixty-thousand actors living in Los Angeles. How disconcerting. No wonder I can't get a job. Which reminds me...if you really want to see stars, go to the Hollywood unemployment office. And get in line."

STAN
Give us another excerpt.

ROBERT
This is an illustration of what happened to us when we were in the studios. Years ago a friend Phyllis had gone to college with came into town with a gaggle of small Brownies in tow. We were working at Universal Studios at the time and arranged to do our part by showing the kids around the lot, ending with lunch at the executive commissary. But before we went in to the dining room we told them, "The actors eat here so they won't be bothered. Don't ask them for their autographs or tell them how much you like their movies. Promise?" Eight or ten small heads nodded solemnly. We took them inside, led the way to a large table, looked around and no one was following us. All the Brownies were standing in a small crowd next to a table where Gene Barry (of *Bat Masterson* and *Burke's Law* fame) was sitting. As promised, they weren't asking for his autograph or saying a word, but all those big, round eyes silently watched every bite he took.

STAN

Beautiful, Bob. I have the book and it's terrific. Norma, what are you doing now?

NORMA

The memoir is being published, as I said, later in the spring. And I've just finished another novel, called *Cremona*, which is about four days I spent in the city of the violin makers; Stradivarius, Guarneri, Amati. I went there with my cousin to help him to do some research on a historical novel he wanted to write about Guarneri, and we found that what he wanted to write just didn't take place, it couldn't have taken place, and he couldn't write his thing. Meanwhile, I discovered the mystery of the violin, which I'm not going to tell now because I want people to read *Cremona* and find out how the violin came to be and how and why the city of Cremona is the center of violin making, which is something even Yehudi Menuhin never found out before he died and he wanted very much to know that. But I did the research and it's a terrific book.

STAN

I want, in our remaining minutes, to find out the secrets of putting a piece together. Whichever of you wants to take the lead on this.

ROBERT

In our case, we've done several books like this. This latest one is about Hollywood and Los Angeles. We've done previous books. Our last book was about San Francisco. It's a matter of, one, to have the credentials. Whatever you're going to write about. If it's going to be a novel, it's a great help to have a really great story. If you're writing a non-fiction book like ours, why should people believe you? You need to write about something that you know, that you have some expertise in the field. We wanted to write some travel books, so we went to travel publishers and we had been writing travel articles for ten or twelve years for travel magazines and newspapers. We had a real background in the field. So when we say to them that we have an idea for a book, it's this, they'll listen to us. So the thing to do, if you're going to write a non-fiction book at least, is pick the thing that you know. If you work in a bank, write about how a bank works. Everybody knows something. Write about that.

NORMA

The memoir, that was something I knew about intimately. Not only that, but Abe Polonsky, who was a blacklisted screenwriter, said, "Norma, you're telling these wonderful stories about what happened in France, Picasso, Sophia Loren, Ingrid Bergman, all these people you knew. This has got to be recorded, this is history and this is something that needs to be written. I think you should write a memoir. And also, non-fiction is very popular now, memoirs are very popular and you are really fitted to write this. You've got to tell it, but you've got to be honest. You've got to really tell it and if you can't be honest, don't write it." So I sat down and tried to write it honestly, with all the bloody details, things we knew about. Sophia Loren, who became our dear friend, and her husband, Carlo Ponti. We made a picture with Ingrid Bergman. All these things and their private lives are in there as well.

STAN

So, Bob, I should just sit down at the typewriter and start writing about Stanley Dyrector and his memories?

ROBERT

No, you should sit down at the typewriter and write a ten-page proposal that says what this book is going to be about and why people would want to buy this book, that you're writing, rather than some other book in the field, something that's special about the book you're going to write and then write a couple of sample chapters. And you send this proposal out and if the first publisher says no, you send it to a second publisher.

NORMA

Or you get yourself a very good agent and you send your proposal.

ROBERT

Getting a good agent can be more difficult than getting a publisher.

NORMA

Even if you have an agent, you have to do what Bob says. You have to do a very good proposal and sample chapters, maybe three chapters well done, to show what you can do.

STAN

My thanks to our guests, Norma Barzman and Robert White.

Chapter Six

THE STANLEY DYRECTOR SHOW

Tonight's Guest
OLIVER CRAWFORD
Film/Television/Novelist

STAN

Hello, ladies and gentlemen, and welcome. I'm your host, Stanley Dyrector. Our guest, Oliver Crawford, is an icon among the creative people of the film and television industry. His writing career has spanned from the Golden Age of television to the present day. Ollie has written movies, live-action dramas, and comedies for such fondly-remembered shows as *Rawhide*, *Star Trek*, *Ben Casey*, *The Fugitive*, *Gilligan's Island*, and more. This versatile craftsman has been a story consultant for *Iron Horse*, starring Dale Robertson; *Medical Center*, starring Chad Everett and James Daly; and also *Madigan*, starring Richard Widmark, and other hits. Ollie's awards include Emmy nominations and a Writers Guild nomination for an *Outer Limits*. He is the winner of the National Conference of Christians and Jews Brotherhood Award, for a *Death Valley* script. A novel he wrote, called *The Execution*, was made into a television motion picture.

Oliver Crawford was also one of two hundred writers blacklisted during the infamous McCarthy period. He is among only ten percent who recovered their careers. Ollie has also been the only member of the Board of Directors of the Writers Guild of America/West to serve an unprecedented twenty-six years.

Ollie, are you a graduate of Princeton or Harvard or Yale, to accomplish this great body of work?

OLLIE

No, just the college of hard knocks out of Chicago.

STAN

Well, let me ask you this: Did you always want to be a writer?

OLLIE

Well, as far back as I go, or can remember, I've always wanted to write. But I had other talents, so to speak. My mother was a fine artist and I at one point had a scholarship to the Art Institute of Chicago. And at one point, during the Depression, I was a commercial artist. And then I wanted to become an actor.

STAN

Tell me about that. I love actors.

OLLIE

I think the talents link. You know, somebody does one thing, usually you can do another. And then, at the same time that I received a scholarship to the Art Institute in Chicago, or shortly thereafter, I received a scholarship to the Goodman Theatre in Chicago.

STAN

Hey, that was a very important group.

OLLIE

Well, that's still a very fine organization, equivalent to the New York Theatre Academy, the Cleveland Playhouse, Pasadena Playhouse. In my class, at that time in the very late '30s, were Karl Malden, Sam Wanamaker, Geraldine Page, and a number of others that have gone on to make their mark.

STAN

Those were real heavyweights.

OLLIE

Yes, ace actors. However, as things balanced out, I moved little by little into the writing aspect of it and got a little lucky at the outset.

STAN

Who gave you a break?

OLLIE

Well, listen, no man is an island. Somebody has to take an interest. And I struggled like everybody else did right after World War II, and there was a wonderful character actor called Sam Levene.

STAN

Sure, in *Guys and Dolls*, he was Nathan Detroit.

OLLIE

That's the guy, and he was an instructor at the Actors Lab, which was then the preeminent theater company on the West Coast. That was shortly after the War. They were an offshoot of the Group Theatre of the '30s.

STAN

That group included Harold Clurman, people like that.

OLLIE

That's right. Also Elia Kazan, and they produced John Garfield.

STAN

Morris Carnovsky.

OLLIE

And Franchot Tone.

STAN

They were all heavyweights, including Stella Adler and Clifford Odets, too.

OLLIE

And then Frances Farmer. You know, that period produced some very, very strong performers, writers and directors. From Odets came *Golden Boy* and *Rocket to the Moon*. Anyway, they went on to lucrative film careers and they transferred much of their action to the West Coast and started a school. And I remember auditioning as an actor, right after World War II, and my mentors were Sam, Anthony Quinn, and Danny Mann, who went on to become a very good director. He directed *Rose Tattoo* and *Come Back, Little Sheba*, and so on. That's going back a long time.

STAN

Well, fill us in. I want to know about it.

OLLIE

You don't know you were living history until you look back and say, "Hey, that's what happened."

STAN

Did you write at night or something like that?

OLLIE

Well, I took what jobs I could. Of course, my wife worked. She was a legal secretary. We had no children at the time and it was a partnership. And then an agent spotted a play that I had written, a play that the Actors Lab produced, and signed me on and that was kind of the beginning and television was an upstart medium, so there was some opening and the creative juices worked and I began to sell. And it was up sometimes and it was down sometimes.

STAN

So there were lean days and fat days.

OLLIE

That's right, and now it's forty years later.

STAN

Forty years later and you're still here.

OLLIE

Still here and still functioning.

STAN

What is your favorite medium? Is it novels, is it screenplays, television movies?

OLLIE

I believe they're all linked. Your favorite is whatever gives you the greatest satisfaction. The film medium, of course, is primarily a collaborative medium. You have a vision as a writer. Then the set designer, the director, the actors come in, and it may come out completely different than what you had envisioned. The result may come out pretty much the same in the novel because that's totally in your head.

STAN

I want to show our audience a little something from *Star Trek*, and maybe you can tell us a little about it, since you went in at the beginning of that.

OLLIE

Yes, I'm one of the original writers on the original series of *Star Trek*. And I did four of those.

STAN

And that was when?

OLLIE

It was in mid-'60s. It only ran two years, that's all, although it seems like more. At the end of the second year, it was canceled. (Star Trek ran three seasons.) But it was brought back on a summer rerun and it just picked up. And the Trekkies have kept it alive. And I'm sure that the NBC executive that canceled that show is probably selling shoes somewhere today.

STAN

I'm sure the Trekkies and many others will recall, and can probably still recite, the opening scene of *Star Trek* , with the voiceover: "These are the voyages of the Starship Enterprise. Its five year mission: to explore strange new worlds; to seek out new life and new civilizations; to boldly go where no man has gone before." And your credits for the show include the teleplay of "Let That Be Your Last Battlefield;" the story (written with David Gerrold) for "The Cloud Minders;" and the teleplay (written with S. Bar-David) and story for "The Galileo Seven." It must be great to have been part of that show.

OLLIE

Well, not only that but the fact that it still replays and it began over twenty years ago, and it's nice to get the occasional residual.

STAN

Oh, so they're still paying off?

OLLIE

In so many forms, it's a cash cow. You know, no matter what they do with it, it's a sure money maker in terms of pictures and so on. It's just one of those golden ideas that Gene Roddenberry had tapped, you see.

STAN

Besides doing that particular show, which is obviously a classic, you did *The Fugitive*, and you did so many other shows, like *Madigan*, with Richard Widmark, with top flight actors and producers.

OLLIE

That's correct. As I look back upon my career, beating back the competition, so to speak, meeting the competition, getting idea after idea, I really wonder why there wasn't a burnout. Although there always is a time when you think you've had your last idea and you've sold your last story, and you really don't know if you'll ever get another job. But in every field, you know, there is an aristocracy that just keeps rolling and there's another plateau of people who get things on, and another third plateau, which is just doomed to disappointment.

STAN

But how do you get an idea and how do you nurture it?

OLLIE

Well, first of all, it's like the old Hungarian axiom as to how you make an omelet: first, you steal two eggs. So I steal two ideas. It's what you see on other shows; it's an exchange with people; it's what you read in the papers, and your own juices. And it's a constantly changing field. It was a little more intimate in the old days, because you actually met one-to-one with the producer. And I usually used a formula, went in with three ideas, figuring one would take, or feed the story editor, or the producer, and they'd come back and by the end of the session, we'd generally come to an agreement as to what we wanted to see up on the screen. Today, it's largely staff written and there are so many people and so much input, to me that's the reason that there is so much that's bad that's come out of a committee approach—even if there may be some that's good—as opposed to the one-to-one that I think was prevalent and I think is much better.

STAN

Taking a cue from that, I want to talk to you now about a television movie that you wrote, based upon the book which you also wrote, *The Execution*. That movie had some pretty heavyweight actors.

OLLIE

Yes. We had Loretta Swit, Rip Torn, Jessica Walter, Valerie Harper, Barbara Barrie, and Sandy Dennis, who has unfortunately passed away.

STAN

Oh yes, that was really a loss because she was a marvelous, organic actress who really brought reality to the film. The voiceover preceding the beginning of that movie was pretty powerful, talking about five women, all victims of a Nazi sadistic torture years ago, now all alone in their quest for justice and revenge and how the police won't know, their husbands won't know, and even they won't know who commits the execution. This is a tremendous piece of work, *The Execution*. You put in years of your life on it, and then you, as the craftsperson, were able to see it go on the screen. Now, was there a difference in the transition from your writing the book to it's being seen on the screen?

OLLIE

Oh, absolutely. The genesis of this is a true story of five women, much later in life, who met in Los Angeles after they'd served in a concentration camp. They did not know each other then. They met subsequently by chance circumstance, and thought that they had encountered their tormenter who ran the camp, but he'd already served time for other crimes and therefore could not be tried again. You needed new evidence; it's many years later and there's just no way of catching up with him. And they concoct this scheme of their own to get rid of him when they can't convince the authorities to go ahead. Very decent people, wonderful women and yet they commit this act, this moral act, so to speak. What I had written and I'd hoped to see on the screen was older women in the present period, but the NBC Network, in their wisdom, said, "No, let's make them younger women" and they set the story back in time, as if it made any difference. I think it would have had more punch, if they'd had a cast of older, kind of sloppier-looking women, rather than these gorgeous ladies . And I think that took away a little bit from the reality, you see.

STAN

But it was, Ollie, a marvelous film on TV.

OLLIE

Well, this is an occupational hazard with writers. We sell material and never quite see fulfillment, or constantly complain. Like, Joseph Wambaugh, you know the list. Recently, Ann Rice, with *The Vampires*, was so unhappy with Tom Cruise. That became very public and she has since recanted. You don't know whether that's publicity or not. But it's why many writers have become directors and producers.

STAN

So they can have some control over their own work.

OLLIE

Absolutely. That's correct.

STAN

But let me throw this at you, Ollie. You have such a background, but there was a time when you were blacklisted in this business.

OLLIE

Oh yes. In the early '50s, when I was a young, upcoming writer, at the age of thirty-three, it looked like I was on my way. And my background included my having had certain political beliefs, having supported certain organizations, for instance, the Committee for the Protection of the Foreign Born. When my parents came over, around World War I, they didn't have government handouts, you know. Your family or friends took care of you, those that preceded you in immigration. And this was one committee that was formed and they helped. I remembered this many, many years later and made donations to that group and many others, and later, they were labeled communist and, of course, during the great scare of that period, that was the cornerstone of our foreign policy, the defense industry, and everything else.

STAN

For people just helping people, right?

OLLIE

That's correct—and even if you had a link to someone who wrote a check, you were in deep trouble. It was a terrible period. The House on Un-American Activities came to Hollywood three different times, I think, '49, '51, and 1953. By 1953 they had already been through all the stars, you know, Larry Parks, and John Garfield and Eddie G. Robinson and so many others. They were scraping the bottom of the barrel to get to somebody like me. Nobody knew who I was. But why did they come out? Because the producers were bending over backwards, furnishing them with starlets and such.

STAN

Is that right?

OLLIE

Well, they didn't go after the furniture makers in Grand Rapids, Michigan, did they? And the furniture makers wrote checks too, and dentists in New Jersey wrote out checks to these organizations, but the Committee kept coming back to Hollywood. Richard Nixon was a prime mover behind this; he used it as a launching pad for his career, as did so many other politicians.

STAN

You were working for Hecht-Hill-Lancaster at that time, weren't you?

OLLIE

Burt Lancaster's organization at that time was the largest independent organization of the time and he was a major star. I wrote the only picture that Burt directed.

STAN

Which film was that?

OLLIE

The film was called *The Kentuckian*. I was called in at the time by the producer, who said that they had information about my involvement, political involvement, and that I would have to go before the House Un-American Activities if I wanted to clear my name. Otherwise, I would be rewritten and my name taken off the movie. And I had a big dilemma: do I become a stool pigeon? The Committee wanted the names of other people, in different organizations, and I decided that I couldn't do it. And believe me, it cost me a lucrative career. I was offered a picture, another picture deal. Well, anyway, the point is, 'to thine own self be true.' My wife, bless her—my late wife, unhappily—was thoroughly cooperative and she said, "You cannot save this family by exposing another family to this kind of disaster." And somehow, I endured, went into exile. I was a political pariah in my own country, but I came out of it. I lucked out.

STAN

And you're a survivor, a total survivor.

OLLIE

Yeah, but you know, it hit some people pretty hard.

STAN

There were people who committed suicide, people who never worked after that.

OLLIE

And now, we have a different problem. Now, fellows like myself, who've been around a long time, you know, we have to contend with ageism. I believe that I have the vitality today that I had thirty years ago. But I'm dealing with people much younger and my contemporaries are either retired or deceased and I'm getting much too much respect out there from the survivors. I had an experience, with a retired producer who told his son— a producer on a TV series who's still active, so I won't mention his name—he ought to get a writer for his show and that he had to talk to Ollie Crawford, who would give him a fine show. So

I walked in, and instead of the one-to-one relationship that you used to have with a producer, or the story editor, which you'd come out of with some understanding, there were about four or five different people, as if they were acting like buffers. If someone got too enthusiastic, somebody pulled it back. So it was kind of a defensive situation. But the producer's son, whom I knew, said, "Mr. Crawford, we're so happy to see you." And the moment he called me "Mr. Crawford," after forty years of being called Ollie, I knew I was in trouble.

STAN

So how do you look at the world now? Do you look at it differently than you did when you were a fledgling tadpole, as we say?

OLLIE

Well, as I grow older, I know less. I was pretty opinionated as a young man and I was very gung-ho and eventually I have come to the point where I somewhat despair. I think we've come to a time in our country, or the world, where we've discovered our resources are finite. And I think there's going to come a time when we've got just too many people using up too many resources and we're going to be unable to replenish.

STAN

And what are we going to do about it?

OLLIE

Write about it. I've written. I've completed a novel, which I'm sending out to publishers, and I'm dealing in the future, looking to what we can be able to do. It's a highly fictional story, but based upon projections of what life will be fifty years from now.

STAN

Give us a little preview, Ollie, of what you think the world might be like fifty years from now.

OLLIE

I'd like to but I think in the publishing world, the film world, you don't give out an idea it's taken you a long time to write and nourish. You've got to forgive me if I get suspicious. And the point is, everybody feeds upon everybody else and I'm no exception. If I hear a good idea or read a good book, I say, "My god, how can I put a spin on that, so that it's original?" You know, we all do this.

STAN

Well, that's good to know. We all want to learn something and that's why we have the wisdom of gentlemen like yourself.

OLLIE

Well, I don't necessarily know whether it's very flattering to be called an icon or to be told that I'm wise. I just kind of lucked out. I've also had an aspect of my career where I was an actor. I appeared in two Broadway shows, both of which were flops, but great experiences. At one point, as I said, I wanted to become an actor but it didn't work out. My writing took precedence, I think. I must tell you a very funny experience. Right after World War II, I got a veteran's ten-point advantage. The government said anybody who's a veteran can apply for any government job and get ten points over anyone who did not serve. And I took a postal exam and I scored over one hundred because I got ten points. I think I got ninety-two and with the additional ten points, it was 102. And in the meantime, I'm pursuing a double career. I'm trying to write and I'm trying to act and not quite making it. And the Post Office called me about jobs and after the third time, they threatened to take me off the employment list if I didn't take the offered job. So I took it. I wanted to make a living, you see, in the meantime maintaining what contacts I could. And I was assigned to the Westwood area, delivering mail to people whom I couldn't get in to see on interviews. And I'll never forget—the producer is still alive, although retired, so I won't mention his name—-I knocked on his door and on some pretext or other, handed him the mail rather than just leave it, and tried to engage him in conversation. I don't think he was quite happy about it, you know. And then he finally said, "Well, you'll come and see me at my office." And then I went and saw him at another time and he says, "The only reason I'm seeing you is you took a novel approach. You got a lot of chutzpah." So that was just one of my exciting adventures.

STAN

We're almost at the end of our show, believe it or not. The time has gone fast and we're wrapping it up now.

OLLIE

It's gone that well and that fast. Next time I'll interview you.

STAN

Oh well, I wouldn't mind that. But before we go, what can you say to future writers out there?

OLLIE

If an idea grips you, if you feel you have something to say, write it. And don't let anybody tell you that you can't, or that it isn't any good. You know, in due time you'll come to your own conclusion as to what the material is.

STAN

That's it, ladies and gentlemen, you heard it first here, from Mr. Oliver Crawford You go for the gold no matter what, because you got it in you. Am I right?

OLLIE

That's right.

STAN

We concur. And on that note, we conclude our show with many thanks to Oliver Crawford.

Chapter Seven

THE STANLEY DYRECTOR SHOW

April 14, 2001

Today's Guest
ROBERT LEES
Screenwriter

STANLEY

Hello ladies and gentlemen, and welcome to *The Stanley Dyrector Show.* You know, we have one heck of a guest and one heck of a show. The gentleman we're going to talk to today is Robert Lees, noted screenwriter. He won two Oscars -- one for Pete Smith, Short Subjects at MGM, called *Penny Wisdom*, and one with Robert Benchley.

But before we get to that, let me tell you a little bit more about Mr. Robert Lees – who was also a blacklisted writer in Hollywood – and for years he couldn't get work. And so we're going to talk about that; we're going to talk about how he wrote *Lassie,*and how he had such a big career. First, I have to ask: Robert Lees, how did you become a writer?

ROBERT

Well, I guess truth is stranger than fiction on this, Stanley. I wanted to be an actor – probably as you did - and wound up being at Metro - Goldwyn-Mayer during the Depression. I left UCLA because of the Depression. And my father had some kind of a friendship with the Rapf family at MGM and through those connections, I got extra work, bit player work. I danced in *Dancing Lady*.

STANLEY

You were a dancer?

ROBERT

Well, not a very good one. I tried to do a time step and couldn't handle it and I tried stuffing my shoe, incidentally, to make myself taller, to join the chorus and I stuffed it with toilet paper and when I tried to show my time step, the shoe flew off, the toilet paper came down like a streamer and the dance director says, "What the hell's going on here?" He says, "You're too short and you can't dance, but if you've got this much guts, I maybe can use you as an associate or assistant." And that's how I got in 'Dancing Lady'.

STANLEY

You danced with Fred Astaire, right?

ROBERT

This was Fred Astaire's first picture and nobody knew much about him - he came from New York – but the guys in the chorus knew all about Fred Astaire. Metro let him go, as you may recall, and he went to RKO. They didn't know what they had, he was so good. And after he danced with Crawford, making her look good, the guys in the chorus said, "Fred, show us what you can do." And he danced for the chorus. And they said, "My God, this man's magnificent." But Metro-Goldwyn-Mayer didn't understand that.

STANLEY

But how did you become a writer?

ROBERT

Oh, well – I decided I had to get myself a screen test and I got the opportunity, so I wrote a test for myself.

STANLEY

You mean as an actor, you wrote a screen test?

ROBERT

I wrote a test to be showing what a great actor I was.

STANLEY

And were they impressed with your great acting?

ROBERT

The result was they said, "The acting was lousy but the test was well written." So the result of that was I became a junior writer at Metro-Goldwyn-Mayer for I think about three years or so. And they had other junior writers. One of them was Fred Rinaldo, who came from Dartmouth. And we got together in the Junior Writer Department, which was completely abandoned, because nobody wanted to buy a writer who was earning $35 a week to do a big picture for Metro-Goldwyn-Mayer when they could get Ben Hecht or somebody. The hell with that. So Fred and I became a team, and we managed to get into the business doing a thing called *Chain Letter Dimes* for Pete Smith. That was the craze at the moment, chain letter dimes, so we wrote a script overnight and hoped maybe they would accept it – which they did – and that got us in the Shorts Department and we were there for three years and did thirty-five shorts.

STANLEY

Is that where you won the Oscar?

ROBERT

Well, *How to Sleep*, with Bob Benchley, won the Oscar one year. Then *Penny Wisdom* was for Pete Smith. But we did thirty-five of these things. We did a lot, about seven, Benchleys. We went to New York on Benchley's request because he said, "I'm a drama critic. If you want me to do some of those shorts," he says, "send the boys to New York." So we were put up at the Algonquin.

STANLEY

Is that the Algonquin, the fabulous hotel the famous Roundtable was?

ROBERT

The Roundtable – Benchley.

STANLEY

Dorothy Parker.

ROBERT

Dorothy Parker and Donald Ogden Stewart. Well, here we were, young kids, in the hotel with a suite and Metro-Goldwyn-Mayer paid for everything. I'd never been to New York before.

STANLEY

You're from San Francisco originally?

ROBERT

Correct. So here was the wonderful situation of being in New York, writing for Bob Benchley at the Algonquin, and we had carte blanche to go to the William Morris Agency with anything we saw on shows, that Pete Smith could maybe do, we could sign them up. That was a wonderful three years in that Shorts Department. We did thirty-five shorts.

STANLEY

Were you a contract writer for MGM, writing other things, after that?

ROBERT

No, I don't think we were really under contract in the Shorts Department but we might have been. We were there for three years and never stopped working. And then when we moved up, with Jack Chertok, he said, "I want to do features and you boys now can come with me." He wouldn't let us go early. We worked on something for Joe Mankiewicz, on a couple of things, and while we were in the Shorts Department, we also, in a gym across the way from our office, were doing some boxing.

STANLEY

Oh, really?

ROBERT

And Lucien Hubbard, who was a sports fellow, he did polo and worked with Zanuck, and he said, "Box with me." So here was a producer—and this was a time when we were Shorts Department writers—he ran into my fist; I actually didn't intend to do anything, and it knocked him out. And when he came to, he thought that was rather wonderful, a kid writer knocks out one of the producers. He says, "Have you boys written anything?"

STANLEY

I'll bet you're the first writer to get a job by punching out a producer.

ROBERT

And strangely enough, we had written something, which was really very much like *Grapes of Wrath* or *Lonely in the City,* about the difficulty of a man getting a job during the Depression. And he loved the script and he wanted to do it and Louis B. Mayer said, "It's not politically propitious at this moment for us to do this." Hubbard left Metro-Goldwyn-Mayer, went to 20th Century Fox, where Zanuck said, "You can have anything you want on our shelves that we haven't done." Hubbard said, "I want this picture that I was interested in at Metro." He took our picture and showed it to Zanuck and Zanuck said, "Look, if you want to do this as a B-picture, with a small cast, and it's gonna be a sleeper, that's you. If you want to make a big picture with Henry Fonda and Margaret Sullivan, and so forth, it's my picture and you could be an associate. What do you want to do?" Hubbard said, "I want to do it." Which was the greatest mistake we ever made, we found out.

STANLEY

Why was it a mistake?

ROBERT

Because it would have had a wonderful cast and instead, we didn't. It became a rather forgettable B-picture but it was our first feature picture.

STANLEY

Was that *The Invisible Woman*?

ROBERT

No.

STANLEY

What was it called?

ROBERT

That was called *Street of Memories*.

STANLEY

That doesn't sound like a comedy.

ROBERT

Oh, my God, no. It was a very serious drama about a man who couldn't get a job because nobody knew anything about him. He had been mugged, and he had lost his identification.

STANLEY

Sounds like *Bicycle Thief.*

ROBERT

Kind of.

STANLEY

By the great Italian director, Vittorio De Sica.

ROBERT

I think it was Leonard Maltin who said *Street of Memories* was a great B-picture, but I never saw it and I don't think it played anywhere.

STANLEY

How did you and your partner become a great comedy writing team?

ROBERT

Well, I think mainly because the Bob Benchleys were comedies and most of the things with Pete Smith were. Because Pete, with that dry voice of his - I don't know how many people are still alive who would remember Pete Smith comedies.

STANLEY

They run them on American Movie Classics - In fact, I've seen your show on American Movie Classics.

ROBERT

Well, what's very interesting is that I'm going to be on American Movie Classics, introducing the Shorts Department, because they want to put those things together. So I did a show for them on that.

STANLEY

We have so much more to talk about. How about a little conversation about *Abbott and Costello Meet Frankenstein?* How did that come about?

ROBERT

Well, *Abbott and Costello Meet Frankenstein* I think was the third picture we did for them. We did *Hold That Ghost* and we did something on *Buck Privates*, their very first picture, but we didn't get credit on it. And they said to us, "Look, we have all these monsters and how about Abbott and Costello?" and it was absolutely a funny idea. Already you can see these little comics

being pushed against Dracula and the Wolf Man, and the guy
with the fangs.

STANLEY
Well, Dracula, the Wolf Man, and there was Frankenstein.

ROBERT
Okay, so the whole thing. We wrote the script and Abbott
and Costello didn't want to do it; they didn't like it.

STANLEY
You're kidding, they didn't like it?

ROBERT
The studio liked it but they didn't.

STANLEY
Couldn't they read?

ROBERT
This was to be the biggest picture they'd ever done. And it's
been still showing, as you know, on Halloween and all that stuff.
But I think it was very literate for them.

STANLEY
Really, what do you mean?

ROBERT
Because it was bound, the copy that we did. I mean, the
screenplay was bound in a book, so it was like a published book
and the entire script was there to read, so they wouldn't be able
to screw around with the script like they usually did with most of
their pictures. They were kept to the script, maybe that's why they
didn't like it.

STANLEY
But you wrote funny. How did you know you were funny?
How do you know you're funny?

140

ROBERT

How do you know you're funny? Well, let's discuss humor for a minute.

STANLEY

For a minute, go ahead.

ROBERT

Well, anything that bothers you, and it might be a lot, anything that really makes you afraid or concerned, like the establishment, or death.

STANLEY

Oh, everything you're saying, that's my life.

ROBERT

High and dizzy. So Harold Lloyd falls off a building and hangs on a clock, and people are screaming with fear at the same moment they're laughing themselves to death. So, what you're doing is whistling in the dark, so to speak. So when you get a situation, like a standup comic, if he's black, if she's a woman, if she's ugly, or she doesn't have a good figure; if the guy has a ski nose, like Bob Hope, he makes fun of it. And this is where the humor stands. It's the stretching of the discrepancies in your life, or the shrinking of them, to making no difference, it's so small, which is like a British sense of humor, an understatement and overstatement of what is basically a dramatic situation makes it comic.

STANLEY

And you were getting paid very good money, I might say, to write at that particular time.

ROBERT

Yes, very good money.

STANLEY

I won't even go into what your salary was but it was over a grand, I know, in those days.

ROBERT

Well, when you add the two of us together, we were a team. So if they want Lees and Rinaldo, which is the way we were, as a team, if we were making $1,000, that's $2,000 a week. That's pretty big money.

STANLEY

But then you fell from grace, so to speak.

ROBERT

Oh, did I fall.

STANLEY

And it was a big fall.

ROBERT

Right.

STANLEY

Sterling Hayden wrote a book called *The Wanderer* and there are things in that book that, when you and I spoke, touched you very deeply, you told me.

ROBERT

Very much, and I'll tell you why. When we went to Washington, which was right after the Hollywood Ten, We were the group that was called "The Fifth Amendment." The Ten went to Washington.

STANLEY

The Hollywood Ten; that was Dalton Trumbo, that was…

ROBERT

Jack Lawson, that was Adrian Scott, Ring Lardner Jr.

STANLEY
And they went ultimately to prison.

ROBERT
They went to prison because they did not answer the questions put to them; they were held in contempt; they did not answer the committee's questions. It was really a First Amendment situation. They stood basically on the First Amendment: this committee had no right to ask those questions; it's like invading the ballot box, asking who did you vote for?

STANLEY
Right.

ROBERT
You can't do that. Which eventually they found out they couldn't do and they abolished this committee. It no longer exists.

STANLEY
But Joe McCarthy was so powerful.

ROBERT
Well, Joe McCarthy gave it the name "The McCarthy Period," but the beginning of the Hollywood Blacklist was with the House Un-American Activities Committee.

STANLEY
HUAC.

ROBERT
HUAC. So what happened with the Ten was they were in contempt of Congress. Now, the second group, which was myself and Gale Sondergaard and Ann Revere, and Waldo Salt, a lot of wonderful names. We took the Fifth Amendment on the basis we're not going to self-incriminate ourselves, because at this point, it was incriminating; they already put guys in jail. So our answer was, "We take the Fifth Amendment." Now we could no longer

testify against ourselves. They couldn't ask us, "Who else do you know," to be an informer, for example.

STANLEY

Because the Committee wanted to know who your collaborator was.

ROBERT

Oh, I'll tell you about that. Well, what happened was, when we went to Washington and took the Fifth, the punishment was no longer the committee's punishment. It was the producers'. Cause at the time of the Ten, the producers said, "We will not hire anybody who does not cooperate with the committee." Well, when we took the Fifth and the First, we wouldn't cooperate. That meant we were going to be blacklisted. So the punishment was no longer a fine and a year in jail; it was no longer you could work in Hollywood. So if you were not a friendly witness, you were doomed. You were blacklisted.

STANLEY

So tell us about Sterling Hayden.

ROBERT

Sterling Hayden is now in Washington and he's there and he mentions it in the book; I'm going to read you a few excerpts when I have a chance.

STANLEY

Okay.

ROBERT

Hayden says, "I really am not going to do the job of Larry Parks," who made himself an object of pity saying, "Don't make me crawl through the mud, don't ask me to name names. I'll tell you who I am." The committee said, name names or else.

STANLEY

But they forced Larry Parks. He was really a good guy who didn't want to blow the whistle.

ROBERT

You're so right. So now Sterling Hayden is being brought there, as a big star, to make the committee look good. And the point was that Sterling Hayden, in trying to make the committee look good, became an informer and he said at the time, "I don't know anybody's names in our group of subversives; we only went by first names." Well, it turned out to be the fact, "I do know two:" Abe Polonsky (who's a good friend of mine) and Robert Lees and he gave the names and the addresses and we were coming up the very next day, and our throats were cut. So that's what Sterling Hayden did. And when I started to write some memoirs of what that period was, I came across this wonderful book, *The Wanderer*, in which he says all the things that somebody who informed, I would like to hear them say. And I know Abe Polonsky, who's now dead, would like to hear them say. "What a jerk and what a terrible person I was." If you'd like, I could read you a couple of passages.

STANLEY

In other words, Sterling Hayden said he was a jerk?

ROBERT

An object of horror because of what he did to the best people he knew.

STANLEY

Okay, read.

ROBERT

He says, talking about the room he was in, which was the big hearing room that we all see on television, during the newsreels.

STANLEY

House Un-American Activities Committee room.

ROBERT

No. It was this tremendous room with a lot of people. We were sitting with this crowd of people, and with the cameras, and there was the committee and the guy in the chair, who was Sterling Hayden. And Hayden says, "Above this crowded room, like a mirage, stands a group of people who once were friends of mine. They look at me with grave and saddened faces. No one says a word. I think of Larry Parks, who not ten days ago sat in this very chair and by pleading with the Committee--by begging them not to make him crawl in the mud--consigned himself to oblivion. Well, I hadn't made that mistake. Not by a goddamned sight. I was a real daddy longlegs of a worm when it came to crawling."

And then he says this: "Not often does a man find himself eulogized for having behaved in a manner that he himself despises. I subscribed to a press-clipping service. They sent me two thousand clips from papers east and west, large and small, and from dozens of magazines. Most had nothing but praise for my one-shot stoolie show. Only a handful--led by the New York Times--denounced this abrogation of constitutional freedoms whereby the stoolie could gain status in a land of frightened people." There's a lot more, but I don't want to go into it, because he had reasons for why he informed, because he couldn't get his children, because of his children. A psychiatrist said, "Inform and get it off your chest." He was becoming a big star, where before he was just not much of a man to conjure with. And all these things came together.

STANLEY

Yeah, but Bob, you forgave him. You and Abraham actually forgave a man, and there are many people that would never have forgiven Sterling Hayden. But you did.

ROBERT

Well, we forgave Sterling Hayden for a very good reason. He apologized. He said, "I did a terrible thing." Ned Young, who had been blacklisted, who wrote *The Defiant Ones*, and was an actor: Sterling Hayden had him come to the set and work with him as an important star and had his chair with his name on the back of it, and actually pushed it so that Ned could sit down. Hayden was so terribly just driven by this, he became a drunk. Nobody else did this. Maybe we'll talk about the director.

STANLEY
Well, there's Ed Dmytryk and all these other people.

ROBERT
Well, Ed Dmytryk said, when he turned back after being defiant with The Ten and then decided to inform, "I'm a director," he says, "I have to be on a set. I can't do what you writers can do. You can change your name." Which I did, which you'll talk about later. "Under pseudonyms, you can write. But I have to be on the set and I can't do this. I'm sorry." So he named names and he got back on to directing. Which Elia Kazan did, which you'll get to.

STANLEY
Well, we'll get to Kazan because there's something in *Variety*, also, that you could talk about. It was in *Daily Variety*.

ROBERT
The *Daily Variety* talked about Will Geer and myself, when we were on the stand, and said we "gave a Fancy Dan performance," which was rather funny, cause when I came home that time, after going to Washington and knowing my throat was cut and I'd never work again, my wife met me at the plane and she said, "Oh, here's Fancy Dan."

STANLEY
Fancy Dan who couldn't get a job. And you had a total change in your career. Can you tell us what happened, where you wound up?

ROBERT
Well, I wound up in Tucson, Arizona as a Maitre d'. That was number one. I had two places to go. I had a brother-in- law in the restaurant business, and my brother who was in the clothing business. The restaurant business was my chance to be a Maitre d', because my father-in-law wanted me to go out of Hollywood,

which he thought was a den of god-knows-what iniquity, and go to Tucson, Arizona, where he had taken a place for his health – and bring the kids, his grandchildren. He thought it would be a nice thing to get away from that terrible town which, incidentally, had burned a swastika on my lawn before I left, because I had come from Washington and I'm supposed to be a terrible Red, and we were going to overthrow the government by force and violence.

STANLEY

A guy who wrote *Abbott and Costello Meet Frankenstein* is a threat. I can't believe this country!

ROBERT

I don't blame your hysteria, because it is true. We did nothing but comedies. And incidentally, the producer, when he was called to Washington, actually said he had to watch Abbott and Costello so that we wouldn't throw anything in that would be subversive. It was a crazy time, you know.

STANLEY

A very crazy time. Also, you did something for the Radio and Television Museum, kind of a seminar.

ROBERT

That was later. Cause at this point, I'm a villain along with everybody else.

STANLEY

Oh, right, you're totally undesirable.

ROBERT

Half of my family wouldn't even speak to me, who knew me from the day I was born, because I'm the devil with the horns. It was really amazing.

STANLEY

Wait a minute; you're a Jewish gentleman, aren't you?

ROBERT

I'm glad you called me Jewish and a gentleman; some people don't put those together.

STANLEY

Did being Jewish have anything to do with the blacklist, do you think?

ROBERT

Oh, you asked a very important question. I'd like to answer that one. Yes. I'll tell you why. Neal Gabler wrote a book called *How the Jews Invented Hollywood* and he talked about the fact that there was Goldwyn, there was Mayer, there was Harry Cohn, there were the Warner Brothers, there was Laemmle, all Jewish, and all started off with the early days of the motion picture industry. When the committee came to town, one of the things they did was to ask, like John Garfield, "Oh, what was your original name, Mr. Garfinkel?" You know, they made a point of this.

STANLEY

Julius Garfinkel, was his name, or something like that?

ROBERT

Something like that, and there was another one, Edward Robinson. So they put a lot of pressure on this, because these guys were from the South; they were very reactionary. They were the worst people in the world on that committee. And the producers were very, very conscious of the fact that they wanted to say they were Americans first and Jews second. They did want to say, "We're really Americans, for God's sake." This is the same thing that happened with the Rosenberg trial, by the way: the Judge was Jewish, Roy Cohn, the prosecutor, was Jewish, and they were set up deliberately on this basis because if they set these people free, they would say, "Look, they're Jews, they want to set them free."

STANLEY

These are the supposed atomic spies, right?

ROBERT

That's correct; who were executed. The point being that they said, "Look, We are Americans first and Jews second and this proves it, look what we can do." And Louis B. Mayer and, God only knows, Jack Warner, practically crawled in front of this committee, it was a shameful performance, saying, "We always tried to do patriotic pictures. We don't do these kinds of things - if anything we can do to help this committee, we won't hire any of these people." This is what was going on. And that's where the Jewish situation did come in, very importantly. And I don't know how many people realize the pressure that was being put on Jewish producers to say, "Look, we're not Jewish, we're American." In fact, they very rarely had Jewish characters, they always had the Catholics, they had *Going My Way,* anything but any kind of a Jew; no Rabbis got on the screen.

STANLEY

Let me ask you. You were with Abraham Polonsky, there was an article in the *LA Times,* I believe it was the *LA Times,* about you guys, kind of not very happy that Mr. Kazan was getting an Oscar.

ROBERT

Correct. That was a very interesting protest. The Blacklist was starting to fade. Kazan got an Academy Award for two pictures. Two Academy awards: for *On the Waterfront* and something else. Now he was going to be given an Academy Award for Lifetime Achievement. Well, lifetime achievement included the fact that he informed on his close friends in the Actors Lab, not the Actors Lab but the Group Theatre, and stopped their careers cold. He didn't have to do this to be on the set in Hollywood. He could very easily have worked on the Broadway stage. He took out a full page ad in the *New York Times* saying how great he thought the Committee was and how he never did anything but wonderful pictures that were very American and, of course, went to Hollywood and a big contract. I'd like to point out something which I think is very important: the difference between the informer and the whistle blower.

150

STANLEY
What is the difference?

ROBERT
The informer sacrifices others for the good of himself, while the whistle blower sacrifices himself for the good of others. And you've got a guy like Kazan who was given this kind of money as a whistle blower, which he was not, and not as an informer, which he was, because there was no threat to him for informing. But if he blew the whistle, like what's his name did on *The Pentagon Papers*.

STANLEY
That would be Daniel Ellsberg.

ROBERT
Daniel Ellsberg was a whistle blower. He was a whistle blower and he lost a lot of things when he blew the whistle in *The Pentagon Papers*. But not Kazan; he went to work.

STANLEY
Vanity Fair flew a bunch of blacklisted people, actors and writers, to take a big photo, including such people as Jeff Corey, John Randolph, Marsha Hunt, and who were the writers?

ROBERT
There was Maurice Rapf.

STANLEY
And Ring Lardner.

ROBERT
There was Ring Lardner, who died right after this photo was done; and I'm standing right behind Ring Lardner, by the way, in that picture.

STANLEY
Norma Barzman was also in it.

ROBERT

Norma Barzman; and give me some more names.

STANLEY

Joan Scott.

ROBERT

Joan Scott.

STANLEY

And Abe Polonsky, died unfortunately.

ROBERT

That's correct.

STANLEY

And so, we really have about forty-five seconds. Tell us something about that photograph.

ROBERT

Well, it was a very interesting thing cause *Vanity Fair* decided they would take the last of the living Blacklistees, both actors and writers. They flew out, as you said, people from New York; we were given a fancy dinner.

STANLEY

Walter Bernstein also was flown out too.

ROBERT

Walter Bernstein. Thank you for reminding me. It was a real event and the whole change took place in Hollywood, where we were no longer pariahs, we were great patriots.

STANLEY

You know, we're wrapping up, my dear friend, Robert Lees. I want to thank you so much for being our guest on this show. Let's continue talking as we're going out. If somebody gave you $50 million to do a movie, what kind of movie would you make?

ROBERT

What kind of a movie would I make today?

STANLEY

For $50 million.

ROBERT

I don't know.

STANLEY

Well, in those days, how many movies could you make for $50 million?

ROBERT

In those days, a $1million was a spectacle, Cecil B. DeMille spectacle.

Chapter Eight

THE STANLEY DYRECTOR SHOW

Tonight's Guest:
JEAN ROUVEROL
Author/Screenwriter

STANLEY

Hello, ladies and gentlemen, and welcome to *The Stanley Dyrector Show*. You know, we have a terrific show for you folks tonight. It's a very profound show, I might add. My guest is Jean Rouverol and she was an actress, a hell of a writer, she wrote a book. In fact, she's written six books. One of them, *Refugees From Hollywood,* is a profound piece of work. And we're going to talk to Jean about what happened to her life when she was blacklisted – in our country. But first, I want to ask Jean Rouverol:

Jean, how did you get into show business?

JEAN

Good heavens! Well, I had the good sense to be born to a woman who had been an actress first, then a writer, and had created, had written a play that *The Hardy Family* came from, if you remember that.

STANLEY

Andy Hardy, sure, Mickey Rooney, Lewis Stone as Judge Hardy.

JEAN

Yes.

STANLEY
Your mother wrote *The Hardy Boys*?

JEAN
Not *The Hardy Boys*; *The Hardy Family*.

STANLEY
Oh, *The Hardy Family*, okay.

JEAN
And it was her first, the first play she had go on Broadway. But prior to that, she had followed Alice Brady as Meg, in the first production of *Little Women*. And I just grew up thinking that what you did when you grew up was to be first an actress, then a writer. That was the way it was done.

STANLEY
I mean, you were in a lot of movies; then you kind of made the transition to becoming a writer.

JEAN
Well, let's see: I did movies for maybe three years, a little bit more, some plays. Then I met and married Hugo. We met, by the way, appropriately, at the MGM Commissary.

STANLEY
That was Hugo Butler.

JEAN
Hugo Butler.

STANLEY
Who was a screenwriter.

JEAN
He was a junior writer.

STANLEY
A junior writer; what is a junior writer?

JEAN
A junior writer is like a kind of little group of neophytes, who have qualified by virtue of material they have submitted to MGM and Metro had four to six junior writers every year, a new class of them, and some junior writers made it to, to full writerhood, and some didn't. And I followed Hugo, actually, as a junior writer some three years after he was a junior writer. And I met him when he was there at Metro. Waldo Salt was one of his buddies.

STANLEY
Waldo Salt, who won a couple of Academy Awards for *Coming Home* and *Midnight Cowboy*.

JEAN
And I had done little theater up in the Palo Alto, San Francisco Bay Area with Waldo. So I came down already knowing Waldo.

STANLEY
Right, right. You know, we have a couple of photos I'd like to show. I am holding up the Federal Bureau of Investigation report on you. And it's about, what, 500 pages? Can you tell us just a bit about what it is?

JEAN
That I sent for under the Freedom of Information Act, and it took me about, oh, about two or three years to get it. And when it came, it was practically all blacked out. If you flip through the pages, you'll see that almost every page, it's just black, black, black ink, "for security purposes." And I tell you, you cannot believe, and I'll tell you about what a blameless life we were leading in Mexico when they, while this stuff was being regularly invented.

STANLEY

Right, right, they were just keeping tabs on you guys. Golly, they knew everything, they knew where you were.

JEAN

They thought they knew everything. They were inventing and supposing.

STANLEY

But they knew you had six kids, right?

JEAN

I think they did, but I tell you, as often as not, they would get Hugo and his son, Mike, mixed up.

STANLEY

Oh, really?

JEAN

When my son went off, transferred from Columbia to UCLA, they thought it was Hugo who had enrolled at UCLA, and sent an agent hotfooting out to see what he was up to up there. I mean it was that kind of wild misinformation.

STANLEY

It was because of who was heading the FBI at that time.

JEAN

Yeah, I guess, I guess.

STANLEY

I mean, a lot of things have changed.

JEAN

And the climate was Cold War.

STANLEY

Cold War climate, right. Now this was when you were under contract to?

JEAN

Under contract to Paramount. I was the first person to have a deal at Paramount, an acting contract that allowed for six months off so I could go to college and six months on, so I could act in movies.

STANLEY

That's a dream situation.

JEAN

I worked with Norman Foster in *The Leavenworth Case*, for Republic. That was, gee whiz, I think I was earning something like $75 a week for doing, being the lead of a movie. We did it in two weeks; no overtime, either.

STANLEY

Two-week wonder.

JEAN

Yep.

STANLEY

You appeared in a radio drama, *One Man's Family*.

JEAN

One Man's Family – I was on for about thirteen years. I played Betty, the wife of the youngest boy, Jack. I was the one that had 6 children on the air. I remember telling Carlton Morse that I wanted, I had always wanted to be an actress, a writer, and have six children – and by golly, I did.

STANLEY

Your dreams came true.

JEAN

The only thing I didn't take into account was the possibility of a Blacklist.

STANLEY

Yeah, well, that was a terrible thing. Let's talk about your journey to Mexico.

JEAN

Cleo Trumbo took photographs on our flight from the United States down to Mexico. Dalton Trumbo had already served his jail sentence for contempt of Congress. He was out, but like the rest of the Hollywood Ten, he was very afraid that he and his fellow former jailbirds were going to be re-subpoenaed and asked the same questions as before by Congress and indicted on a brand new charge of contempt. He had gotten out of jail in spring of 1951. Hugo and I were already on the run by then. We hadn't left the country yet. We wanted to, quite badly; we had four children at that point. Not easy; it's never easy to duck a subpoena with four children. I don't recommend it.

STANLEY

You know, reading your book, I got panic attacks while reading about these incidents.

JEAN

Trumbo also wanted to get out of the country, because he was just terrified but he couldn't leave until he got some money together. He had to sell the ranch that he lived on, to have any money to go to Mexico. But he had been doing some reading and he knew that there was a good school down there. He and his wife had three kids. And ours, of course – our four. And we were interested in the fact that our kids could get a decent education wherever we went.

On the way down, we stopped at the volcano of Paracutin, a brand-new, newly-born volcano.

I had our year-and-a half year old daughter, Emily, with me at that moment – maybe she was two. And I was staying in the car and she was asleep in my arms. The others traveled ahead on donkey-back. I knew that traveling on donkey-back, to look at a volcano, with a one-and-a-half to two year old child in your arms was a perilous trip.

STANLEY

I'm sure.

JEAN

So I didn't make that particular one. Anyway, we got to Mexico City, and the Trumbos got one house; we got another. We'd had quite an adventurous trip down, because there was a traveling strep working its way through all Trumbo kids and all the Butler kids. So it took us almost a month to get down.

STANLEY

Wait. Before you got to Mexico, there's a little story in your book.

JEAN

Yes.

STANLEY

About how you got a visitor at the house.

JEAN

Oh, yes.

STANLEY

Let's backtrack a bit.

JEAN

Let's backtrack.

STANLEY

To when you decided to leave the country, and tell us a little piece from *Refugees From Hollywood*.

JEAN

Okay. Hugo and I at this time were working on a little domestic comedy for Hecht-Lancaster; Harold Hecht/Burt Lancaster; at Columbia, which was subsequently released as *The First Time*, with, Barbara Hale. Hugo heard that his friend, Waldo, had gotten a subpoena the night before.

STANLEY

Waldo Salt.

JEAN

A new roundup, a whole brand-new roundup. At this moment, the guys are still in jail, the Hollywood Ten, and Hugo, dressing for work the next morning, decided that he'd better not come home that night just in case. "I've tried the army," he said, "and I know I wouldn't like jail." So he had elected to have dinner at a restaurant with his agent and a couple of our non-Red friends and perhaps to sleep away from home, which is why I, in turn, was eating alone with the children in the dining room that night when we heard the doorbell ring. I knew with absolute certainty who was outside. And sure enough, when I looked through the peephole in the door, I saw what I was afraid of: two men with hats, standing under the porch light. Now, as anyone who's ever lived in Los Angeles knows, no Southern Californian ever wears a hat unless it's raining. Those two men might as well have been wearing placards. They didn't identify themselves, however; they merely asked for Hugo Butler. I said he wasn't in. They asked when he would be. I said I didn't know. They asked where he could be reached. I said I had no idea. Things seemed to require some sort of amplification. "We've had a little disagreement," I said, improvising wildly and frightened to the point of tears, "and I don't know where he's gone or when he'll be back." The two men looked at each other, clearly unconvinced. Then they shrugged, said they'd be back, and left. I closed the peephole window and tried to think what to do. If they had our address, they must have our phone number too, and our phone might be tapped. So I couldn't phone an alert to Hugo, at least not from here. I went back to the dinner table. Not to eat – I couldn't, my heart was pounding too hard – but merely to give the visitors time to leave the neighborhood. I asked our housekeeper, Sarah, to put the children to bed, filled a couple of laundry bags (to legitimatize my departure in case anyone was still lurking outside), called a cab (they might know our license-plate number), and went to an all-night Laundromat a few blocks away to drop off the laundry and call the restaurant from a pay phone. I asked for Hugo, and in a moment he came on the line. "Honey," I said. "Get on your horse." There was a pause. "No shit," he said.

                         STANLEY
    Were you a communist?

                         JEAN
    Yes.

                         STANLEY
    And why were you a communist?

                         JEAN
    Well, I was actually on leave, a leave of absence at that moment because I had resigned when Hugo went into the Army. The Party gave their members leaves of absence when they joined the Army. The Communist Party was so gung-ho about the war that they didn't want any American Red to feel any sense of conflict between the Army, his duties as an American soldier and…

                         STANLEY
    Being a communist?

                         JEAN
    And being a communist. So they gave them leaves of absence. And when Hugo got out of the Army, it was actually our third child that got him out and when we had our third child, he became eligible for discharge.

STANLEY

So he fought for our country. He was a loyal American. What I don't understand, is why would you become a communist in the first place?

JEAN

Okay, okay. You have to look at it historically. Hugo and I had both been through the Great Depression, the Stock Market Crash and the Great Depression, and it looked to us as though capitalism had feet of clay. We couldn't see anything very good or very dependable about capitalism. Dictators, Hitler and Mussolini were gradually taking over Europe. We could see fascism on the rise there. Spain had fallen. The legitimate, democratically elected government of Spain had fallen to Franco, and to troops and supplies that Hitler and Mussolini had supplied him with. And nobody was doing anything about it; nobody was upset except the Communists. Also, there were serious problems in the United States, we felt. The trade union people were being bitterly persecuted. Joe Hill had been shot.

STANLEY

Joe Hill? Who?

JEAN

There is a famous song: "I dreamed I saw Joe Hill last night" – one day, you'll find it out…

STANLEY

Hm. Okay – sure.

JEAN

Pete Seeger sang it – anyway, it was just a bad time and it seemed to us that communism at least provided a few answers when nobody else was offering any.

STANLEY

Interesting.

164

JEAN

So we joined – mostly you were having coffee klatches at peoples' houses once every couple of weeks and discussing Marxism philosophy.

STANLEY

Is that so? Didn't know that.

JEAN

I mean, it was kind of nice. They were like college bull sessions.

STANLEY

Oh, sorry. I am not up to the inside of how things were.

JEAN

And you felt a great fondness for your group.

STANLEY

Did you ever feel like you were subversive, that you were against America?

JEAN

No.

STANLEY

You just wanted what?

JEAN

Communism was on the ballot, had been on the ballot.

STANLEY

Oh, so it was legal then, the Communist Party?

JEAN

It was legal then.

STANLEY

Oh, I didn't know that.

JEAN

It didn't become a dirty word until the Cold War.

STANLEY

You mean in the 1950s?

JEAN

Yeah, well, no, in the '40s.

STANLEY

In the '40's – before, it was legal. In other words, if you were a communist, it wasn't against the law or anything like that?

JEAN

Then suddenly there was a rash of states declaring it illegal and there were, there were – Oh, the Florida Little Smith Act had not been implemented until then – But then, oh later on, I think in the early '50s it was implemented. The Smith Act itself, that is to say. Anyway – and the thing that frightened us most was the passage of the McCarran Act.

Now, the McCarran Act was passed during the height of the Cold War. That is to say, probably '46 or '47, and that gave the government the right *in times of war or insurrection* – and we knew, we knew who would be doing the defining – the government had the right to intern, quote "suspected spies or saboteurs." And we heard, there was a rumor, that they were refurbishing the Japanese relocation centers for us, for people like us. And, I do believe that if there had been the kinds of demonstrations to the Korean War that there were subsequently to the Vietnam War, we'd have been out of there. Anyway, it was the notion that the United States had, as far as we knew, concentration camps, that made us very anxious to leave the country. We felt that the United States had so changed that it didn't resemble the country that we had known growing up, loving.

STANLEY

Also, I think there's another issue that we have to touch upon and that issue was ratting on your friends.

JEAN

Well, the fact is that the Hollywood Ten would not have minded declaring their own affiliation.

STANLEY

With the Communist Party?

JEAN

With the Communist Party. But once you said, "I am or I was a communist," then you had no right not to answer every question about who else was a member. The Fifth – that's the Fifth Amendment – the Fifth Amendment gives you only the right against self-incrimination. You cannot refuse to incriminate anybody else.

STANLEY

So why didn't you stay here and assert the Fifth Amendment then?

JEAN

The Fifth Amendment at that time hadn't been tried. Remember, at that moment the Smith Act had not yet been passed, so it hadn't been proven that it was a crime to be a communist. So, incriminate yourself, incriminating yourself for what? It wasn't clear legally that we could be incriminated, that we could be incriminated in any crime.

STANLEY

Right, right, right.

JEAN

Also, we knew that we would certainly be blacklisted forever, if…

STANLEY

You'd never make a buck!

JEAN

Yes. You'd never make a buck anymore. And Hugo and I had both grown up in the industry. We didn't know how to do anything else.

STANLEY

Right, right.

JEAN

And we knew that the First Amendment didn't work; we knew that the Fifth Amendment had all kinds of hazards. And it was just better to get out. And so we fled.

STANLEY

I know that you spent ten years in Mexico. And there are so many wonderful incidents in your book. But, you know I want to ask you: As you were living in Mexico, didn't you get the realization that the Soviet Union was the crapper? I mean, it was the worst. Stalin was a bum.

JEAN

Until 1956, who knew? I mean, we were convinced – sometimes there would be rumors and we were both convinced that they were spread by the FBI and the CIA, that it was part of the Cold War. And when we first heard about the Khrushchev revelations at the 20th Party Congress, it was rumor. There was never – Khrushchev had apparently convened, privately, after almost the expiration, the end of the 20th Party Congress, he had convened a private meeting only of the Russian communists – not of the communists from anyplace else in the world – only the Russians. And he had begun to tell them, in something like four to six hours, had told them hour upon hour upon hour, about Stalin.

STANLEY

Purges?

JEAN

Purges, the anti-semitism, the…

STANLEY

Anti-semitism – I want to touch on this. Are you Jewish? Did you have to be Jewish to be a communist then?

JEAN

No, no, no, no.

STANLEY

So it wasn't only Jews who were communists?

JEAN

No, no, no.

STANLEY

Okay, I just wanted to know.

JEAN

In fact, in fact, Trumbo wasn't any more Jewish than we were. Hugo was one-eighth; that was as much. He couldn't have made it under the Nuremberg Laws.

STANLEY

Okay, so now you're living in Mexico. You have four kids, then suddenly you find out you're pregnant.

JEAN

At first there were four children. Mike became a screenwriter eventually. Susie teaches still photography back East and she has just published her first book, called *The Hermit Thrush Sings*; it's a lovely book. Mary was a poet in college and is a teacher now. Emily ended up as a librarian and is a teacher now. We were living in a house built by Juan O'Gorman, who designed that wonderful library building and built that nine-story-high mosaic in University City.

STANLEY

One of Hugo's movies that he did while you were in Mexico was *Torero*.

JEAN

Well the first picture that he did was *Robinson Crusoe*, with Luis Bunuel. The second one, he fell in love with bull fighting and he made a documentary called *Torero*, and did some of the directing. He did the narration and it was released under a *nom de plume*, he was Hugo Mozo.

STANLEY

Hugo Mozo?

JEAN

Mozo means house boy in Spanish. And *Torero* eventually was nominated for an Academy Best Documentary Award, under the name of Hugo Mozo.

STANLEY

Really.

JEAN

And I think that, somebody named Ronny Lubin, who happened to know where we were, said to the audience that was viewing it, "That's really Hugo Butler."

STANLEY

You know, there's an interesting piece in your book, where you were expecting money from the United States and you were pregnant at the time, and the postman, a humble postman, helped you out. Can you tell us a little bit about that one character?

JEAN

This was in very early 1953 and we were expecting this baby. We had gone down to Mexico with $17,000; that was our grubstake. Now I don't know how much Trumbo had. He didn't have much more, 'cause he had to go home after a while. We had gotten down there by the end of '51, late in '51, and by early spring of '53, it was gone. And Trumbo took our possessions and his own down to the national pawn shop called the Monte de Piedad to hock 'em.

STANLEY

Right, right. But eventually you had to wait a couple of weeks.

JEAN

We had – in the meantime, while Trumbo was doing that – Hugo and I were writing our family and good friends, asking for loans up to $500, for which we would give them part of Hugo's share of Robinson Crusoe. We sent the letters off; no answer. Nothing, nothing comes. We telephone Hugo's mother. She said, "But, but – there were several checks," she said, "I sent them last week - airmail." No sign. We were frantic. We just didn't know what to do. And we realized that they were probably, had probably been stopped. We learned later that the counsel for HUAC, for the Congressional committee, had been down, and one of the Congressmen, had been down to Mexico, and been talking to the Mayor. So they had probably asked for our mail to be monitored.

STANLEY

Right.

JEAN

But in the meantime, we didn't care about that. We just wanted the checks in the mail, because we needed to eat. And that morning we had to borrow money from our cook, Ramona, our beloved cook.

STANLEY

Ramona, there's a wonderful story about Ramona, who you brought to Italy with you when you left exile.

171

JEAN

And then to the States. Bless her, bless her. In the meantime, we had to borrow money from her to buy the groceries one morning. So when the mailman came, I went out to talk to him, 'cause I wanted to know if he knew anything about the missing mail. And he looked very embarrassed and he said, "Well Senora, it's algo, como es. . ." He said something to do about it's being monitored, it's about being *revisado*, being read. And I said, in my bumbling Spanish, "I don't care about its being read. We just need the checks." And here I am, I'm out to here and he's just looking so upset. So he says, "Come talk to my supervisor." And I take our littlest child, Emily, down to the Post Office, when Mr. Sanchez? – I've forgotten what his name is – was going off duty.

STANLEY

Right. You were pregnant.

JEAN

Eight months, eight months pregnant.

STANLEY

Right, but the Mayor, I mean – they did give you the money, they did give you the checks?

JEAN

Well, there I was with my daughter and the dear mailman, and the dear supervisor, who was equally sweet. And the mailman said, "La senora esta enferma," meaning "she's ill," which is his nice way of saying she's pregnant. And I told them I'd had to borrow money from our *cocinera* so that we could eat that day and I knew there were checks in the mail and we didn't know what to do about it.

STANLEY

And they fixed it up, right?

JEAN

The supervisor said, "Senora, I'll see what I can do." He was terribly embarrassed. I go home, I tell Hugo what's happened and I don't think that anything is going to happen and I go upstairs to take a nap and I'm ready to weep. And in a few moments, I hear the mailman's little whistle and things arrive.

STANLEY

And the checks were in the mail.

JEAN

The checks were in the mail.

STANLEY

And we're on our way out, Jean Rouverol. I'm sorry. I love you. I mean, it's gone – I wanted to mention *Lylah Clare* that you wrote. I wanted to mention *Autumn Leaves*. I love that movie, *Autumn Leaves*, with Joan Crawford, Cliff Robertson. That was a real romantic movie. And also poor Hugo and how ill he was near the end, because he'd been given that prescription of what, amphetamines?

JEAN

Amphetamines, yes. Methedrine. His doctor thought that it was a way of – Hugo was suffering from fatigue, not surprisingly. We'd had a second baby by then.

STANLEY

And that was Rebecca.

JEAN

Yeah, it was Rebecca. He was tired and the doctor thought the methedrine was non-addictive. He thought it was a stimulant that was non-addictive. He was feeding it to Trumbo at the same time.

STANLEY
Wow.

JEAN
Trumbo made quite a lot of enemies while he was taking that stuff.

STANLEY
Thank god those days, those years are over now, although you did gain a great deal in Mexico, didn't you?

JEAN
You end up poor but I would not have missed those years in Mexico for anything in the whole world.

Chapter Nine

The Stanley Dyrector Show

1999

Our Guest Today
BERNARD GORDON
Screenwriter/Author/Producer

STAN

Hello, ladies and gentlemen, and welcome again to *The Stanley Dyrector Show*. We are indeed proud to have as our guest screenwriter, author, and producer Bernard Gordon. Here are a few of Bernard's credits: *55 Days at Peking, The Day Of The Triffids, The Thin Red Line, Hellcats of the Navy*, starring Ronald Reagan and his future wife, Nancy Davis Reagan. Isn't it ironic that Bernard Gordon, who was blacklisted during the McCarthy era, wrote the romantic love lines of dialogue in that movie for our former President and Nancy? Bernard has written a book about his life and times, called *Hollywood Exile*. But before we get into that book, Bernard, I really would like you to tell us how you became a writer. I know you were once a private detective.

BERNARD

I really want to talk about my book, which just came out and which I'm selling. How I became a writer: I was a story editor at Paramount Studios for seven years, until 1947, when there were the first hearings in Washington for what became known as the Hollywood Ten, before the House Un-American Activities Committee. Somebody there named me as a communist sympathizer and shortly after that, after seven years of work at Paramount, I was terminated in December, just before Christmas and just before my wife and I were to have our first child. I had to make a living somehow and therefore I decided the easiest way to go was to become a writer and I started writing, as a screenwriter. That's how it happened.

STAN

But you were also a detective.

BERNARD

That detective thing seems to fascinate you and it's true that it was interesting, but that only happened some years later, after I became blacklisted and again I was looking for a way to make a living. A friend said that he was going to start up a system of being an investigator of accidents. Mostly it involved what we called fender-benders. You'd go out and take pictures of the cars and skid marks and get police reports. You had to get witness statements. It was very dull. But I did have one criminal case, involving a young black man in Bakersfield, California, who was accused of raping a white woman. And I had to go up there and try to help get him off, which I did with the help of a marvelous black attorney from here in Los Angeles. So I became a detective for a few years and then, fortunately, I began to become a blacklisted screenwriter, somebody who was called in to do work under another name, and that's the story of how I got into being a blacklisted writer. But how I became blacklisted is something else, if you're interested.

STAN

I am very interested and our audience is interested. And the name of your book is about your blacklisting.

BERNARD

Thanks for asking. The name of the book is *Hollywood Exile: Or How I Learned To Love The Blacklist*. It's kind of an ironic joke, because I not only became blacklisted and went abroad to work, but I had a very successful career working in France and

Spain, making some rather big pictures, and finally wound up even running a movie studio outside of Madrid, Spain. So I had a really wonderful time in spite of having been blacklisted, which is not true, of course, of most of the blacklisted people. I was fortunate. Maybe I had a little talent, maybe I had a few breaks, and that's why I said I learned to love the blacklist. So, what were we talking about?

STAN

I want to hear more about your writing career. I have a manuscript of your book, and I'm looking at these other movies that you did, like *Circus World, Battle of the Bulge, Custer Of The West, Krakatoa East of Java, Bad Man's River, Horror Express, Pancho Villa,* starring Telly Savalas and Anne Frances, *Surfacing,* starring Joseph Bottoms, and *Cry of Battle, The Thin Red Line,* starring Keir Dullea and Jack Warden, based upon the novel by James Jones.

BERNARD

That's right. I was working in Spain for a man named Philip Yordan, who was very well known in Hollywood and had more than fifty screen credits himself. Some people said he ran a script factory. He happens to be a friend of mine and he gave me very good work and very good pay during the very bad blacklist years. So I don't want to badmouth him, because I really respect him and like him. But he had ways of picking up books and things at bargain prices. James Jones' novel, *The Thin Red Line,* which is a thick, five-hundred-page book, which followed his writing of *From Here To Eternity,* which perhaps some people will remember and which became a very successful film, was about the battle for Guadalcanal and was strictly a war story. It had no women and it had no love story; it was a narrative and didn't have a dramatic function. But Yordan had to make another picture, so he threw the book at me and said "Let's see if we can get a script out of this," and I worked on it for quite a long time but I finally got a screenplay and we did go to work shooting the film for practically nothing. We were working in Spain at the time. We had Keir Dullea and Jack Warden, that was about the entire cast, and we had to save money.

STAN

Later on, in recent times, that was remade into a multi-zillion-dollar movie.

BERNARD

That's right. Just this year, or maybe last year, it was released. It was made in Australia by a famous director for either $50 or $60 million—but $10 million doesn't matter anymore these days. The picture I wrote was shot in Spain was shot for $300,000, and I must say that some people like my version better because it's more of a straight, honest-to-god war story. The only silly thing in the story is that the producer was married to a very pretty young girl and he had promised to make a movie actress out of her, and he wanted a scene with her in the movie. This was after the picture was shot. I said, "What is a girl doing in Guadalcanal in the middle of one of the worst battles in the war?" He said, "Oh, well, the guy is dreaming of her or thinking of her or remembering her or something." I wrote a dozen different scenes to try to get it done. They finally shot one of them and there she is in the picture. If you look at my book, you'll find a photograph of her with Keir Dullea, and many of the critics, who liked the picture actually, said they didn't know what this Yordan lady was doing in the picture and neither did I, even though I had to write it.

STAN

Well, you can't fight the producer. Actually you can, but you usually don't win.

BERNARD

What was typical of making that picture was when the troops got off the ship and had to go marching into the island, I had them going through a patch of mud, to show some reality, and the producer said, "Mud? You can't walk these soldiers through mud. Their uniforms will get muddy and what will happen when we have to have them cleaned? How long will it take? Or we'll need another set of uniforms." No money on uniforms, no dirt, no mud. So that was it, no mud, and that was typical of the way the movie was made.

STAN

You mean they wouldn't go for having the uniforms cleaned?

BERNARD

Well, that costs money and we had to save money. That didn't affect the fact that we had a pretty good personal story between the two principal actors.

STAN

You said that James Jones' novel was basically a narrative. But *The Thin Red Line* preceded Francis Ford Coppola's *Apocalypse Now*, which was based upon Joseph Conrad's narrative in *A Heart of Darkness*.

BERNARD

Well, there I am, beating Francis Ford Coppola to the punch. I must say that I was a little nervous about how James Jones would feel about what had been done to his book, but I met him in Paris. I was invited to his home and we had a wonderful evening drinking and he said, "Oh, what the hell. I got $25,000 for the picture and I built this beautiful bathroom with beautiful wallpaper and it paid for it all, so I'm very happy."

STAN

Bernard, you're a very modest guy, so I've got to bring out certain facts. Your liberal leanings were really the beginning of the film industry's fair treatment of blacks and other minorities. You were the one who wrote in parts, particularly for black actors, because there were no parts for black actors, or not many, I should say.

BERNARD

Well, it's so true that blacks were ignored in those days in motion pictures. As a matter of fact, even a producer who wanted to put a black actor in had trouble because of the conditions in the South. In my first film, my first script I should say, that I was working on after I was fired in 1947 as a Red—I'm not just a liberal, I'm a Red—one of the things I tried to do was to create any kind of a part for a black actor. My partner and I wrote in a black taxi driver in a meaningless scene, but at least they would have to hire a black actor to play it. When the producer read the scene, he asked why we put the word "black" in there, why was the taxi driver black. We were prepared for this and we said it was realistic, it gave atmosphere, it was proper, it was true. He crossed out black and said we couldn't have a black in the script. I asked why and he said it would only make trouble when they tried to show the picture in the South. And that's what things were like in Hollywood and in America at that time, and it's a very serious matter and it's not a joking matter. My wife, who was the Executive Secretary of the Hollywood Canteen during World War II, had to fight the problem of black soldiers, sailors, marines—who were there dancing at night with hostesses of all kinds—dancing with white hostesses. This created a problem and the motion picture industry didn't want this to happen. They finally worked it out by establishing that a hostess could refuse to dance with anybody at all, whether he was white or black or pink or sweaty or hairy or tall or small, but the refusal was not to be on the basis of race. This was the policy that was accepted.

However, there was a big Marine MP who didn't like this and would take the black soldier or sailor into the men's room and beat him up if he was caught dancing with a white woman. And my wife, Jean, and Bette Davis, who was the president of the Canteen, had to go down to the captain in charge of the Navy and tell him that they wanted to get rid of Mickey, the MP who was beating up the blacks, and nothing much was done. But the point is that during those four years, when there must have been a million servicemen who went through the Canteen, there were thousands every night in different shifts, they did see blacks and whites mingling together, sometimes dancing with each other— that is, black men and white women—and socializing in a way that was unheard of before the war. That's the way it was. It shocks people today to know that there were two musicians local unions—a black one and a white one. They could not even have the same union. I don't remember the numbers of the unions, but a man named Baron Morehead was the black head of the black musicians local and there was another musicians local for the whites. They did not come together. That's how bad things were. Today, they're not perfect by any means, I'm not saying that they are, but they have changed a good deal since those days.

STAN

Bernard, you were blacklisted and, from reading your book, I know there was a lot of pain and suffering, and there must have been a great deal of suffering by your wonderful wife, Jean. And you raised your daughter, Ellen. And you took your wife and daughter overseas. Can you give us a take on Jean leaving America?

BERNARD

I'd like to read my dedication to Jean; it's very short. It says, "To Jean, wife and closest companion for over fifty years, who knew all the bad times and supported us with good cheer though her own wish for a peaceful and settled life was never realized." Jean had worked very hard; she had been through the Depression, like most of us of our age, and she'd suffered a great deal. And when she finally got through working for four years, seven days a week, and seven nights at the Canteen, all she wanted to do was have her child, settle down, be a wife, be supported, and there I was, starting to be a screenwriter and it looked good, and then I was blacklisted, so she had to go back to work. It was a very tough times for her. But mostly, when things started to get better, and I got this opportunity to go to work in Europe, we had to pack up and leave America and leave our home and go and live first in Paris and then in Madrid, which doesn't sound bad and it wasn't bad. But it was not her idea of what she wanted to do with her life. It was very rough for her. So, there it is.

STAN

And Ellen, your daughter?

BERNARD

My daughter, Ellen, at the age of nine or ten, was taken out of school here. At first she was put into a little school in Switzerland and then she went to the English School of Paris and the American School of Paris, and the American School of Madrid, constantly shifted around, always losing her friends, always having to make new relationships, and it was very disturbing for her even though now she looks back on it because she speaks several languages and she remembers a lot of interesting things that happened, but growing up for her was difficult under those circumstances.

STAN

I recall reading in your book about your and Jean's concern about Ellen answering the door because of subpoenas. Can you tell us a little bit about that?

BERNARD

That was early on and I had just finished working at Universal, where I wrote my first two films. One was a Tony Curtis film, one was a Rock Hudson film, and you can read all about that in the book.

STAN

I remember the Tony Curtis film, in which he played a deaf prize fighter. I watched that film at the Loews Pitkin in Brownsville. I loved that movie.

BERNARD

How much did you pay to get in? You probably sneaked in. That film was called *The Flesh And The Fury* and that was the first film I wrote and the first credit I got.

STAN

And *The Lawless Breed* was the Rock Hudson movie, right?

BERNARD

Good for you, I can't come up with all these titles. I was supposed to get a contract because they were so happy with my work at Universal. This was 1952; almost everybody else was blacklisted. I had not yet been subpoenaed because I became a writer late in the game, so I was not known by the stool pigeons who talked to the House Committee on Un-American Activities, and yet somebody did inform them that I was a Red and my producer sneaked and told me that there was a subpoena out for me. So I was fired from Universal and went home and watched while the marshal sat outside the house in his new Oldsmobile waiting to try to serve me a subpoena. My little daughter, Ellen, at four, liked to run to the door when the bell rang and open the door and be welcoming to everybody, naturally. We were ducking the subpoena because we thought that if we didn't get subpoenaed, maybe we wouldn't appear before the Committee, maybe we'd fall through the cracks, maybe we wouldn't become blacklisted. So we tried not to accept the subpoena, and therefore we weren't answering the door for the marshal. We had to tell Ellen something about why she shouldn't continue to answer the door and be such a cheerful receiver of people coming to the house. so we lied. We said, "Ellen, this man is trying to sell us magazines and we don't want the magazines and he's a pest and a nuisance and we don't open the door for him," and we stopped her from going to the door. She bought the story but twenty years later, when she was married and working with some other people who were by no means political but were also being subpoenaed for other reasons, she finally put it all together and said, "Oh my god, they lied to me when I was four and that was what was happening." That's the story of my daughter and the subpoena at the age of four.

STAN

That's just a wonderful story. Ellen loved it overseas, didn't she? You got her a horse, I remember reading in your book, an Arabian horse. You were a good father.

BERNARD

It worked out that I was finally making $1,500 to $2,000 a week and that kind of money in those days was good. The dollar was worth ten times what it is today, and in Spain and in France and Europe, it was worth twenty times as much. So I was really rolling in money. We had a magnificent apartment, over 3,000 square feet—it was called seigniorial—we had a car and chauffeur, we had two live-in maids. I was living fine, that's why I say I learned to love the blacklist. And Ellen, like so many little girls, was in love with horses and horseback riding and we were able to buy her this beautiful white Arab horse and keep it in a stable and all this cost practically nothing in terms of our dollars at the time. She became an expert rider in dressage and won many medals and awards. And to this day, although she doesn't get to ride much but does ride occasionally, she remembers those days with great pleasure.

STAN
Bernard, there's so much to cover and so little time. I recall reading in your book that when you were a producer, Telly Savalas thought you were Mr. Money Bags. Can you give us your take on that?

BERNARD
We had a lot of fun when we were making these films, *Pancho Villa* and *Horror Express*. The set was up on the hill and I was down in the office building and the dressing rooms down below. Every once in a while I'd get a frantic call from the director saying that the scene wasn't working, we have to do something, please help us.

I was the producer at this point, not the writer, but I was an experienced writer, so I would write a new scene for them and send it up and tell them to shoot it. And they would just shoot it, because the boss told them to shoot it. And the next day, there it would be in the screening room in the dailies. And I was able to see whether what I wrote was any good or whether it lay there like a dead fish on the screen. It was veryeducational for me. But Telly Savalas came to me one day and said, "You know, Bernie, you're the luckiest man I've ever known in the film business." I said, "Why is that?" He said, "Not because you're rich" —he assumed that since I was running a studio, I was a rich and powerful man and getting a lot of money, but the truth was I was working for expenses and promises, although I didn't want to tell him that— "but you're the only person I've met in the motion picture business who can say, here's the scene, shoot it and we have to shoot it. And the next day, we see it. That's very unusual; it hardly ever happens. You're very lucky and very smart." So Telly and I got along fine.

STAN
What was the most difficult film you did overseas?

BERNARD
They were all difficult, it's hard to single one out.

STAN
You had to be multi-lingual, didn't you? You worked with Spaniards, with French men, with Italians. How did you communicate with these people?

BERNARD
Communicating with the Americans was the most difficult. When we were doing *55 Days at Peking*, we had terrible problems with the actors. David Niven was signed to do his role as the British ambassador long before there was even a script, because Sam Bronston, the producer, met him in the Grand Hotel in Rome and was a big shot and said he wanted him to do this picture and signed him for $300,000 and David Niven agreed. And when David Niven came to work after the picture had actually started shooting, I was on a one-week vacation for the first time in several years because the hotel doctor had told my boss that I was running a fever and he had to let me have some time off. My boss, Philip Yordan, asked me whether I really wanted some time off and I said I did. He asked me what I would do and I said I would just go to a beach somewhere and get some sun. And he asked me what I would do on the second day. His idea was that anyone who would want to spend more than one day on the beach, not working and not making pictures, was crazy. Anyway, there I was in Monte Carlo enjoying my time on the beach, and after two days I got a frantic call from Yordan in Madrid, telling me that Niven had come to work and was refusing to do the picture because he didn't like the script. Yordan said he wasn't telling me to leave my vacation and come back to work, but if I didn't, we would be in terrible trouble. So I broke off my vacation and came back.

I asked Yordan what he wanted me to do and he told me to write him "a Hamlet scene." What he meant, and what I quickly understood, was give the man a scene where he says, "Am I right, am I wrong, am I doing the right thing keeping these people here?" I wrote this self-searching scene and, sure enough, Niven read the scene and agreed to do the picture. That kind of thing went on constantly. Later on, Charlton Heston thought he had a right to have some complaints, too, and I was working on another script when Yordan came to me and said shooting on the set had stopped because Heston didn't like the way things were going and insisted on having a new scene. I asked Yordan what he wanted me to do and he told me to just quickly give Heston a new scene, a scene with a child; a kid in the picture always works. I didn't even have time to dictate to my secretary; I was just sitting at the typewriter, banging it out, and Yordan was standing over me, pulling the pages out of my hands. I told Yordan not to show the pages to Heston yet, because I hadn't even read them myself, and Yordan said he wouldn't, he would just talk to Heston, but Yordan did show them to him and Heston liked the scene and they went on making the picture. We had similar problems with Ava Gardner. This kind of thing went on endlessly and it gave me a condition where I ran a temperature for many months on end, because the pressure was unrelenting.

STAN
At that time, were you the producer and the writer?

BERNARD
At that time, I wasn't a producer. That came years later, when I was put in charge of a small studio that was opened outside of Madrid. First, I was working on Bronston and Yordan films at the main studio in Madrid.

STAN
Time is wrapping up here. I wanted to ask you, what did you like best, being a writer or a producer?

BERNARD

I loved being a producer. It was a small studio, but nevertheless, there I was, king of the hill and everybody deferred to me. I was always surprised that when I would walk on the set, things suddenly stopped and everybody looked to see what the boss was going to say. I wasn't accustomed to this and I would try to be friendly and look around, and on one occasion, on *Horror Express*, I said, "The lock on the case is different than the one you were using yesterday. Why is there a different lock?" Well, they had goofed and had a different lock and we couldn't do anything about it. Nobody had noticed it in the film.

STAN

I want to thank my wonderful guest, Bernard Gordon. I really want folks to get his book, *Hollywood Exile*. I read it and loved it. It will give you a real insight into the humanity of a wonderful man, Bernard Gordon.

Jeff Corey with Stan Dyrector

Chapter Ten

THE STANLEY DYRECTOR SHOW

2001

Tonight's Guest
JEFF COREY
Actor/Teacher

STANLEY

Hello, ladies and gentlemen, and welcome to *The Stanley Dyrector Show*. Today we are indeed privileged and honored to have as our guest Mr. Jeff Corey, the noted actor/teacher. Now, I could go on for fifteen days telling you Mr. Corey's credits. They are just phenomenal credits. He was in *Butch Cassidy and the Sundance Kid*. He was in *Wake of the Red Witch*; he played Mr. Loring in that one, I believe. He was in *Home of the Brave* and he was so magnificent opposite James Edwards, it is a movie historical moment. But I have to ask our esteemed guest, Mr. Jeff Corey, Jeff, how did you become an actor?

JEFF

Well, I hated school work but I did very well in my high school, in New Utrecht High School in New York, and they decided to put on a version of Goethe's *Faust*. They needed a Mephisto; they'd been waiting for several years.

STANLEY

That's the devil, right, Mephisto.

JEFF

Mephisto, yeah, who had some very good colloquies with the Lord. And Mephisto's thought was that God was somewhat blinded by Faust, the old man, how honorable he was, and I wanted to prove that he was just a charlatan, just like everybody else. So, Mephisto was right. It turned out that Faust became a whore monger —and his lady, Margarita, was with child when she descended to heaven and was chastised. So I became very popular in my class, and the girls began to like me, I was such a good actor.

STANLEY

New Utrecht High, that was Brooklyn?

JEFF

Yes. With a bevy of Bensonhurst ladies. I graduated and I didn't have the grades for City College or Brooklyn College, so I worked for a week for Singer Sewing Machine, trying to sell needles and Singer sewing machines for six futile days. And it was depressing. I said, "What am I going to do with my life?" Then I happened to pick up a postcard saying that I had an appointment to audition for the Milward Adams Scholarship, a two-year Scholarship, at the Feagin School of Dramatic Arts. So, I went there and I did young Treplyov in *The Seagull* and I did Malvolio in *Twelfth Night*. One of the teachers, Hugh Miller, was stuck in America; he was doing plays in America because there was a depression in the United States and in England. But he really loved my work, so he wanted me to win this scholarship. He was very excited about me. And then I began to do a play, it was an A.A. Milne play, about detecting, and I played the detective. And I began – now that I was acknowledged as this great actor who won this nationwide contest—I began to use my stentorian voice, and he said, "Dear boy, you've just got to stop that. Every time you talk, it sounds like you gotta, like you need to go to the toilet." And he chastised me and I began to act well there. And two years later, when we broke for the summer occasion, I felt it was time to get a job. During the Depression, my parents gave me a quarter every day; 10¢ for the BMT, a nickel each way, and for

15¢, I managed to get some sort of nurture, so I felt I ought to go to work, so I got a job in a factory. We got $6 a week to work for six days. Straight time, overtime, but if you had more than two hours overtime, they'd pay for your meal. So, we were making signs for beer. The Volstead Act had just been nullified, so liquor was now legal and we were working on window signs for things like Pabst, words we'd never heard of, because I grew up not knowing anything but near-beer.

And one day, Franklin Delano Roosevelt, they said, was going to pass quite near us. The factory was on 13th Street and Fifth Avenue, just a short distance away. And I asked, because I spoke English well and all that, and all the guys in the factory with me said, "You talk to the bosses and see if they let us go off." So I went to the bosses and I said, "At a certain moment, Roosevelt will be walking, will be driven down Fifth Avenue, with Al Jolson, the great person, vaudevillian and singer." He was going to precede the Prez and the bosses said, "Not at all. You guys stay at your work benches." So the nascent radical in me said, "Hey, wait a minute, wait a minute, guys," and we had a conspiracy. At the right moment, we all walked down there as Roosevelt, the handsomest visage I'd ever seen, and Al Jolson went by. We were so excited. And then we went back to the work benches. And I must say the bosses did not say anything.

STANLEY
Did you get your first professional role soon after that?

JEFF
My first professional role came in a circuitous way. I still was not an Actors Equity Actor but I worked on the Works Progress Administration. Wait a minute, wait a minute, that's later. John Houseman and Leslie Howard were looking for young men to play spear carriers in their production of *Hamlet,* and I did it with zeal. And then when we went on the road, there were some changes in the cast, an English actor by the name of Greene and another, Joe Holland, who was playing Horatio. Greene took his role and Leslie, being of a democratic vision of the world, said, "All these spear carriers, I want them to audition for the part of

Rosencrantz," which was made vacant. And I won. And on the 2nd of January 1936, I got my Equity card.

STANLEY
So you were a professional actor and getting paid money.

JEFF
That's right. I was playing Rosencrantz. At the age of twenty-two, I was playing Rosencrantz and we toured the United States and Leslie wanted to tour all over the country, because he knew people liked his work and he was so grateful to America to have given him such admiration. He was such a big star. And so we played in Globe, Arizona; we played in Denver, Fresno.

STANLEY
Coming to California, coming close to L.A.

JEFF
We came to California and there I was, kind of acting with my equity card.

STANLEY
And you were a Shakespearean actor.

JEFF
I was a Shakespearean actor and I was so proud of myself.

STANLEY
And then you landed in Hollywood?

JEFF
Well, not yet. Someone had told me to get in touch with some people who she knew. And I remember, she took me to Pasadena, and I saw the race track there, and I fell in love with that whole atmosphere of Hollywood. But I came back to New York fortunately, where I met my wife, Hope, and we've been married for 63 years now. In my world, that's a good thing, but it's not that

sensational. If you've got a good thing, you stay with it. I have three lovely daughters and six grandchildren.

STANLEY

That's fantastic.

JEFF

When things were getting bad in New York, after the Works Project Administration was red-baited out of existence. . .

STANLEY

Right, because everybody in it had liberal leanings.

JEFF

Well, yes. Liberal was not a cuss word. Well, not yet. So I was part of a circus act. We did Chekhov's *Marriage Proposal* as clowns.

STANLEY

That must have been a remarkable performance.

JEFF

And I worked with clown makeup and, and our big venue was in Washington Square Park.

STANLEY

In Greenwich Village.

JEFF

Yeah. And then I worked in *Life and Death of an American*, which was a very interesting play, which Piscator, who had worked with Reinhardt in Europe and Bertolt Brecht, he said this was, in his ten years in the United States, this was the definitive, didactic, Brechtian play. Little did we know. Well, when the WPA was done in, sabotaged, I thought, "I want to have a life, I want children, I want a house in the country and I'm gonna go to the Brooklyn Engineering Institute and read, study blueprint reading," because my father had been in the plaster and trim business, which was very difficult during the Depression; there was practically no work for him. And I went there twice and my wife said she had some money in the bank from her mother and grandmother, it was a few hundred dollars, and we had a Model A Ford. She said, "Let's go to California. You talk so adoringly about wonderful California, let's just go." So we got into our Model A car, it was bought at auction at a Street Cleaning Department, and we drove to my wife's father's house in West Virginia and I went to a five-and-ten-cent store and got a brush for 5¢ and 10¢ worth of stove polish. And I painted our drab colored Ford into a very nice black car. And we kept a budget; it took us 18 days to get across the country and our budget reads: 82 dollars and 38 cents.

STANLEY

Wow, that's a real budget.

JEFF

You could get gas for 8¢, you know, and some of the motels were 75¢.

STANLEY

You got here in 1940?

JEFF

1940, and we got off highway.

STANLEY

Route 66?

JEFF

Route 66, which became Sunset Boulevard, and something made me turn to the left and it was Barnsdall Park, it was very attractive. And I saw a sign in a window saying "Bedroom Available," so we paid 3 dollars and 50 cents for this bedroom. We had toilet facilities; we were allowed to do that. And then one day, I wanted to show Hope Hollywood and we rode down Sunset Boulevard and, lo and behold, my eyes caught the eye of Lee J. Cobb and Lee J. Cobb's eye caught me. And, he said, "What are you doing here?" And I said, "Well, Hope wanted to come here and see what the possibilities are in films." And he said, "Do you know . . ." and he gave me the list of all the people who were here from the East Coast, like Jules Dassin, you know, who was recently called by Luc Godard the, absolutely the definitive, great director of our times.

STANLEY
He was married to Melina Mercouri.

JEFF
He wasn't married to Melina then; he was married to Bea. And he was so glad when I called him up. He said RKO had put him under a student contract, director contract and he was working up north, on *They Knew What They Wanted*, that Garson Kanin was directing. He said, "Please come and stay with Bea, she's expecting a child and you can take care of our little boy, Joey, who is four years old." So we had our own quarters within his house; it was marvelous, and they were so glad I was there. And Julie came back to witness the birth of his daughter, Rachel, and then he had to go back on location. There was no rush. And one day I thought I'd try something. I had a Harris tweed jacket and it was in June, and I walked from Vine Street up the hills; I walked, I didn't use the car; I walked to Sunset Strip. And I did what kids did in New York, you go to agents to see who's casting. It was different here. The first guy I spoke to, I told him my credits and he said, "I don't have room for you, kid." The second party said, "Well, I'll think about it." The third party says, "I like you, kid."

STANLEY
I'm gonna make you a star?

JEFF
Just about. He sent me to Metro to see Leonard Murphy, who was head of casting, and I got a day's work in *Bittersweet* with Nelson Eddy and Jeanette MacDonald. One day's work. Then he says, "I want you to go to Paramount." I went to Paramount; they responded to me, and they said, "We got some work for you, kid,

but first we want you to do a coming attraction." It was a picture with, how can I forget her name? The title was *I Want a Divorce*. And that's all I said, and I got fifty bucks for that. In New York, my God, our lovely little apartment in the Village was only $35 a month, and here it was $50 at a time. Then he took me to RKO and he immediately put me to work on a Kay Kyser comedy, which included John Barrymore, all sorts of people. And I worked for a couple of days there, at RKO. And the, since I was at RKO, somehow or other the German director, William Dieterle, who had worked with Murnau, and Reinhardt, Piscator, he saw my name in the Players Directory, it was a fresh copy. And Dieterle, in spite of his enlightened social outlook, still believed in astrology and numerology, and my name fit the right time and without seeing me, I was sent to Culver City, RKO, for wardrobe and then I was told, "At twenty-three minutes after two, be on the set," because the astrological signs were good. So I went there; it's the first time I saw Dieterle and I got the script. I was head of the Farmers Grange and all the other people were older men, very old men. And the very first scene was with Jimmy Craig and Anne Shirley and I was talking, boasting about the Farmers Grange, which was a new thing, and there was a little piglet who was part of a subsequent scene. And they had to shoot the scene, but every time they said, "Action," the little pig would run away. This happened a couple of times and Dieterle was devastated, "What do I do?" I am cabined, cribbed, confined to saucy doubts, like Macbeth says. The property master very quietly went to Mr. Dieterle, and said, "Mr. Dieterle, I think I can help you. Please, please, please. I'm going to be holding the little piglet and I'll high-sign you and you whisper 'action'." So the property master turned over the little piglet and began to stroke his scrotum and the little piglet was ecstatic and we got the scene.

STANLEY

Listen, I have to ask you: *Home of the Brave*, was that before the blacklist or after the blacklist, when you were, like, out of business for twelve years?

JEFF

Home of the Brave was right after I'd got out of the Navy, it was the first important job I had when I got out of the Navy.

STANLEY

You were the psychiatrist. By the way, in the Navy, I just want to briefly say that you photographed kamikaze attacks on the USS Yorktown, an aircraft carrier.

JEFF

And on other ships.

STANLEY

And you won citations from our United States Navy. You were a hero, Jeff. I know you're going to dispute that, but you were a hero.

JEFF

Oh, I'll accept that.

STANLEY

But you were also blacklisted.

JEFF

For someone who was scared shitless, I was pretty heroic.

STANLEY

You could not get a job in this town for twelve years because of that and you became an acting teacher. You eventually became a teacher to many of the great actors in this industry.

JEFF

Well, I never thought of myself as a teacher, but some young people who rather liked my work. There's an appellation, "an actor's actor". It was obvious that actors liked my work, so they said, "Why don't you teach a class?" And I said, "Well, why don't you get some kids, bring them to my house, I'll talk to them," and about thirty kids came, and I said, "I'll get in touch with you when I get a place where we can teach." And Viola Spolin, who later started the Second City, in Chicago, she let me use her studio, gratis. And seven people came. One was Carol Burnett, who I'd gone to UCLA with. The UCLA thing is another story. And the word got out that this was a good class, and I thought it was unfair to keep using Viola's studio gratis, and I got a place near the Technicolor processing place. Like all rehearsal halls, it was terrible. The most awful kind of mohair seats. What happened: they were good kids, it was a good class. But the Hollywood Freeway was being built; you know, the 101. And I had a Plymouth Suburban, which was a very, very good car in those days, which I had bought when I was moderately wealthy. Moderately. And before they went to work, and after they left the job, I loaded my station wagon with 4x5s and plywood and got all the stuff I needed to renovate my garage. I extended it six feet. I tarred the top of it, to make it rain-proof. I put in lights, but the old fuses we had could only take so much. And I had my own studio and that's where the word got out. Then, the class was just doing well. There were some very nice young people. And Jack Nicholson was nineteen. Bob Towne, who later wrote *Chinatown*, and Carole Eastman, who wrote *Five Easy Pieces*, they were all in the class. Jimmy Dean used to sit in on the class. Then 20th Century Fox had a guy who was teaching their contract players how to act, but they didn't like him, so they all came to me. Sheree North, Rita Moreno, Al Adamson, all these people came, Virginia Leith, and it was an astonishing class.

STANLEY

Jeff, I just want to mention some of the things that you have done as an actor. You were in *Star Trek*. {Stanley showed photos on monitor}

JEFF

Star Trek: I was Plasus in "The Cloud Minders."

STANLEY

And you were in *Wild Bill Hickock* and *Little Big Man*.

JEFF
There was an article about that in Directors Guild's magazine, because I did get into the DGA and did some directing.

STANLEY
And you were in *Superman.*

JEFF
Superman and the Mole Men.

STANLEY
With George Reeves.

JEFF
That was the first, the first *Superman* and somebody said– –I'd already been mentioned but I'd not been before the House Committee—"You'd better be careful." He says, "The hell with the House Committee, I want him for the part."

STANLEY
And you did something with John Wayne?

JEFF
That was *True Grit.* And my dialogue was to Kim Darby. I said, "You shot me in my short ribs; that ain't fair." He's just a kind of idiot crybaby. Later, George Roy Hill wanted me for the part of Sheriff Bledsoe in *Butch Cassidy and the Sundance Kid.* And I like to fool around with a part; I knew a good deal about Greek tragedy and the function of the chorus is to warn the audience of impending danger. So when I said to Butch, "Butch, you're one of the finest young men I ever knew" and I spoke to, pointed at Paul Newman, and I said, "You're gonna die," that was really the function of the Greek chorus.

STANLEY
You know, Jeff Corey, our time is wrapping up. A half hour just went by like a minute. And I had so many things to ask you. But let's keep talking while we're going out because you're a

wonderful guest and you have had such a big career and obviously it cannot be fully discussed in a half hour. So we're going to have to do a reprise – is that, is that the word?

JEFF

Boy, I talk a lot, but on a subject I'm fond of.

STANLEY

What was, probably, your favorite part?

JEFF

I don't even think in terms of that. I was pleased that in 1969, I did *Little Big Man, Butch Cassidy* and *True Grit*, all in one calendar year.

STANLEY

And you got along with John Wayne very well, since you also did *Wake of the Red Witch* together.

JEFF

Yes, he liked my acting, not my politics.

Chapter Eleven

The Stanley Dyrector Show

1999

Our Guest Today
JOHN RANDOLPH
Stage/Screen/Television Actor

STAN

Hello, ladies and gentlemen, and welcome to *The Stanley Dyrector Show*. Today we are indeed honored and privileged because we have a great guest. His name is John Randolph. He has been on the stage, screen and television. You name it, John Randolph has done it. He won a Tony for his role in a Broadway show called *Broadway Bound*, by Neil Simon. John's credits include *Prizzi's Honor*, in which he played the father to Jack Nicholson. In *The Execution*, he played the judge. In the John Dean story, *Blind Ambition*, he played the Attorney General, John Mitchell.

John, how did you become an actor? That's what I want to know.

JOHN

Everybody told me that they were interested in how I became one. In City College, I was a student who loved everything social, society, and all that, but I didn't know where the hell I was going. Everybody else in the class knew just what they were going

201

John Randolph and Stan Dyrector

to do when they graduated but I didn't know. I just had a hell of a good time. I loved doing everything – I loved to do acting. But even that, I didn't act at that time. I was just curious about everything. And mostly it was about how people worked and lived and all those things. I was mostly interested in other people, but I also was excited in music and things like that. So I didn't know where I was coming from. And I would say that anybody who ever heard me saying that would realize that that's natural. That's the real thing. But when it's you – you're scared.

STAN
Right.

JOHN
And I told 'em how my brother decided that I should be an actor.

STAN
Your brother was the one that decided that you should be an actor?

JOHN
Yes. He's living in New Jersey right now. But he was wonderful, and I quit – I left class and the day that I left the class, I know that my family would think that something was wrong with me.

STAN
In other words, you left college.

JOHN
Yes, I did. College –what the hell was I doing when right in the middle of it, I decided that I'm gonna go and listen to this – the commercial that was being done, in a place like that TV studio, here, where they were looking for talent on the streets of New York.

STAN
Oh, so you went and auditioned?

JOHN
I went down there, and I never did that before. Because when you're Jewish and you're in education, it's very important you have to keep, you're alive, because you're fighting everything that is wrong as far as America's concerned. But you're doing something. And I was just a young American boy, that's all. And it never occurred to me that something was going to say that you will be an actor someday. I didn't know. I just went down. And my kid brother wrote down, "you've gotta go down for an audition, at such-and-such a time." And I went.

STAN
And how did it go?

JOHN
I tell you, I did not know how to act. I didn't know anything about acting. I had a wonderful time, but I didn't know what the hell I was doing. When I went down there, everybody— old women, young women, and the older guys and everything— everybody was ready to read for the streets of the City of New York – and I was the only one – they were all nervous. I wasn't nervous. I didn't realize that I was stupid enough not to be nervous.

STAN
Well, you were probably a natural. That was it.

JOHN
It was just like I'm talking to you right now. It never occurred to me. But I was interested in history. I was interested in all these things, speech.

STAN
You have played so many varied characters. I remember you played a southerner to Bette Davis in *As Summers Die*. You played Augustus Tompkins, an attorney.

JOHN

Yes. The interesting thing is, you and I were talking before the show about the beginning of my history, and now we're at the so-called end of it, with a great star, and I had no idea that I was doing anything any more important than was necessary, I'm a good actor. I'm proud of it.... I'd really learned a lot of things through the blacklisting and everything else like that. And when we were doing the show with Bette Davis, down South, and we were all of us playing real characters. I played a lawyer who was going to cross-examine Miss Davis. And by this time, I'd already learned that wherever you come from, you have to be honest about it but you have to be able to do other speech patterns. My wife, Sarah Cunningham, was a very big actress and she was from Greenville, South Carolina, and I lived in that area for a long time, and Sarah said[imitating his wife's southern accent], "Now, Johnny, don't try to say anything bad or annoy some people, making bad sounds and talking about things." I said, "Sarah, I know how to do this. Don't forget I've been going with you for a long time." But the point is, it didn't make any difference, because she just – her mother didn't know that. And when I talked to her mother, I would write down, there, "Thank you, Miz Cunningham" and talkin' about her –and I lived in that area for a long time. So I really did an example of something that I myself enjoyed doing. I made more money out of being a Southerner than out of being Jewish. Sarah wasn't Jewish, but more Jewish than me.

STAN

You are an amazing actor. That southern dialect that you just presented is so foreign to from whence you came, isn't it?

JOHN

Yeah. I must tell you it's a bothering thing with a lot of white actors who are told by the people in charge of you, and they thought that maybe you shouldn't be speaking that speech, not the way, John, that people talk. And the director that I had had said, "I think that they don't want you to use a dialect" and I said, "I won many notices with everything I did with this thing." For this particular show that we're talking about – not the one with Bette

–but of the same type. Huff (John's wife, Sarah Cunningham's, nickname), her family reared her nice and easy. Just the sweetest thing. And I sometimes had a terrible habit of saying "I hear they're having a strike down South." Her mother would die when I said that. But sometimes we got kind of dull –but as soon as I said it, everybody just shut up and said, "Now Johnny, have a little cup of coffee and go outside; have something to drink later on, or something to eat. It's a lovely day." They were saying, "don't talk this way." And Sarah was so scared that I was gonna cause trouble, but I moved too fast. I just had a terrible tendency to say, "Listen, I'm a real person and if you think that you know the answers to me" –I'm telling you the way I have worked with people who were the way I am talking to you right now – and it's not bad, it is perfect. And you're not insulting the people. If they think you're making fun of them, that would be different. But I think I made such a living out of being a Southerner, I didn't want to be anything else. Even until I got up to the Irish part of me, then that would be something else.

STAN

Well, let's get back to those early years, when you started out. Eventually you went to Broadway. You did a lot of stage work.

JOHN

In the beginning, it was tough and some of it was madness. For example, once I began to realize I'm gonna go into the service –I was in the Air Force [at war]and I didn't know what was gonna happen. But when I was talking to the people about my background, I began to really try to be things I know. Trying to be a phony doesn't mean anything – it cannot get people. But we're talking now. It's better for me to talk with you this way than it is for some audience. I don't know who the audience is [meaning Stan's audience in TV] but I know there must be an audience there. And I cannot tell if they're twenty years old and I'm eighty-four.

STAN

You are fantastic for eighty-four, let me tell you.

JOHN

I can get out of town quicker than anybody else. It's not just terrible – I loved acting after a while. I enjoyed it. And it was funny –and it was good people. I worked with good people.... Now, I have advice for the actors out there right now, who really want to get into it: I would say, take a chance. If you do what work you think you want to do, go to classes, not talk to other people. But don't say, I don't know how to say anything. I feel like I don't want the young people I know, that they are dead for me, cause I'm a big actor. I don't believe in that. I believe that I've done a couple of bad, dumb shows, terrible shows, without knowing how bad it was, but it wasn't my fault.

STAN

But you stood up, I have to say this, I have to let our friends out there know that you stood up for what you believed in, and you really paid the piper. And you were blacklisted. And I remember seeing a movie, *The Front*, where Woody Allen played this pseudo writer who was actually fronting for the real writer, who was on the blacklist. And, at the end of the movie, I see "John Randolph" -your name- and it said "Blacklisted" such-and-such time, along with Zero Mostel. So, can you tell us a little bit about that particular era?

JOHN

You have some notes here that are interesting [indicating my pad]. I'll tell you one thing: I will fight always against injustice. I don't care. All this crap that people think that there's nobody—I did not work in Hollywood until I was fifty years old. They wouldn't let me work there.

STAN

Because of the Blacklist.

JOHN

I was working on Broadway and thank God for that, because that would keep my wife and two kids alive, and we were just a family. But most of the actors lost their livelihoods and disappeared. A lot of people don't know about that. But I know them. And when there was this thing about the blacklisting, I could talk about that as a truth, because I know what I'm talking about. You got a book there?

STAN

I have a book right here called *Naming Names*, which contains many references to John Randolph. I just want to read one of those items, that "...the actor John Randolph, who denounced the Blacklist whenever he was in telephoning distance of the press, recalls arriving in Chicago, where he was booked for a summer theater performance, only to be told by the manager that a letter from the head of the local American Legion post included . . . a dossier on Randolph and . . . a threat: fire Randolph or we'll picket and shut down the show. Randolph, who had been hit before, assumed the manager might want to call in an understudy, but the show went on as scheduled. After it was over, Randolph said with relief, "Well, I guess it was a bluff." The theater manager set him straight: "Now I can tell you what happened, John," he said. "The Head of our Legion Post is a florist. I called a Teamster friend and told him about the threat. He called the florist and said, "Don't give me any of that shit. You picket the show and your trucks don't roll. So they didn't picket."

JOHN

I'm glad you picked that out. That was a long time ago—that was history for me. That was the breaking of my being blacklisted. I got into a show that played in Chicago and everybody was worried because they said, "Now, listen John, don't say anything to upset people. I thought you should get this job and people are worried that you might say something wrong." I said, "Man, let me tell you something. I'm a guy from New York. I can do anything I want to do and I will not do anything to hate anybody. I will just speak as straight as I can." But I'm gonna tell you something. When I got there, the guy who was worried, who said, "Don't talk about blacklisting or anything like that," was thrilled that I talked that way—because everybody talked about it.

And I didn't care, I was in. As far as I am here and I will be that way.

STAN

Right. I'm sure you stood up for yourself.

JOHN

And I remained. That was the first time that I really had a job where I had a liberal life, had the money. I did work on Broadway, even though the show that I was in was picketed. I thought, "Oh no, my god, that's the end of my life. Now where the hell am I gonna work?" And I had $38 in my pocket; that's all I had. It was during the time of Christmas, and the kids were very young. And I got this job in Chicago and I just found that when I do what I want to do, and tell the truth to people, everything works out. I don't want anybody to ever get hurt. I don't think it's fair, you know, that some people get scared, you know. I don't believe in that. But I do believe that when I come to talk, I just want to talk about myself. If there's a joke in it, then the joke comes out. I have no idea how to do it.

STAN

I know you have come to talk.

JOHN

You really bring everything out of me now, don't you?

STAN

John, you have really stood by so many causes. The Native American Movement. You were there, in the forefront. You remind me of the dialogue that Henry Fonda had in *The Grapes of Wrath*, "If there's an injustice, I'll be there," et cetera.

JOHN

You know how old I was when I heard that? I was going to do a show called *Medicine Show;* it was my first Broadway show. We were never clear about how you do things. When you're young, you know, you're scared. Well, I went to a show with my mother in New York once and they were showing that movie.

STAN

Grapes of Wrath?

JOHN

Grapes of Wrath. I saw it and I thought, "Jeez, what am I worried about? He didn't get any money. He got forty bucks. I better tell the guy who's my director not to worry very much." To me, it was all real, you see. The director became very famous. Anyway, the point is, then I went down to the theater, and I was making up and the director came over—he was an old friend of mine—and he said, "Listen, I hope you're not worried." His hand was cold. I said, "Oh no, Jules, you don't have to worry about things. I saw what happened to the star of a big movie." He said, "I don't give a shit who he is. I'm scared." He was so nervous. And he became a very big director. I don't want to give his name, but that's all true.

STAN

I heard a "Jules," so I'm figuring Jules Dassin.

JOHN

Jules Dassin, that's right.

STAN

The guy who directed *He Who Must Die*, which was, by the way, a script that was based on a book by Nikos Kazantzakis, *Christ Recrucified*. Ben Barzman, another blacklisted writer, wrote the screenplay. John, you have done so many things. In *Heaven Can Wait*, with Warren Beatty, you were the former owner. In *Frances*, you were the kindly judge. That was a Mel Brooks film, his company produced that movie. And you were in *The Adventures of Nellie Bly*, *Tail Gunner Joe*, *Nero Wolfe* (in which you played Lon Cohen). You were also in *F. Scott Fitzgerald in Hollywood*, *The New Original Wonder Woman*, *Columbo*.

JOHN

Well, sometimes they were successful and sometimes they weren't as great as something else. But it doesn't make any difference. What you said is all truthful.[laughter]

STAN

But what brought you to the attention of the Hollywood producers, the big shots?

JOHN

Well, for years I had to work on Broadway. I could not get a job in Hollywood. For me, Hollywood was bad scene, talk. I didn't want to say anything about it but I knew I was screwed. I knew I was not getting jobs. And yet, I had, after the war, I was in a couple of plays.

STAN

Plays, right. Well, in World War II, you were a GI, coming home. You fought for our country, you were a patriot. Were you married at the time?

JOHN

Just before, like every GI, I thought about who am I gonna leave my life to and so forth and so on, and I got married. In World War II, I was against Hitler and I was against the killing of the Jews—I couldn't stand it—so I offered to be in the Air Force.

Ordinarily, I don't believe in fighting, I don't believe in killing, you know, but with Hitler, and everything that I stood for, it was different. I read every book about Hitler. I read everything that I could. I despised anybody who hated other people because of their religion and Hitler was the worst. And I was very honest about how I felt about it. I thought I would be okay, nobody did anything to you in the Army. But when I heard people, GIs, who did say anti-Jewish things, I thought, "Who are these guys? I'm Jewish, man. I know what happened and who are these guys behind me, who are talking like that?" I heard them saying things like, "We're gonna get that little Jew boy." So I wrote to my wife and said, "What do I do about this, how do I handle these guys?

I mean, we're all gonna have to kill somebody, but, Jesus, these guys are scaring me and I want to fight back." And my wife said, "Don't worry about it, Johnny, they don't know what they're talking about. They just tell stories that they think are gonna be smart.... So you have to stand up for what you have to do if you're gonna be in that Army, you better stand up." 'Cause I said, "What if I do swing at these guys? – Or I – trouble!" And when I took her letter and she said, "Johnny, you have to speak up the way you feel." And I said, *"Jesus Christ."* I never expected this nice guy from City College [meaning himself]. It didn't make any difference. Well, I went back to the barracks, and the same guys, Tennessee guys, taller than me, big men and ready to kill –but they were gonna kill others, don't kill me. But I'll take care of those guys at that time. Well, I'll tell you what happened, what really happened, and nobody knows about it except myself. I went to the barracks and again I heard these guys talking like that. And everybody thought these guys were wonderful. They were all regular guys, not from New York. And they started talking about anti-Jewish things and I stopped them. And I said, "Now don't you talk about it like that –what you're doing is something just as bad as Hitler or anybody else like that". Now they're all moving in on me. I forgot that I'm not a gentile; it had never before occurred to me that I was the enemy, suddenly. And I said to myself, "Oh my God, Sarah. Why did you write that letter, because I did exactly what you said and I think I'm gonna be killed." But it worked just the opposite. There was a guy, a great football player from Minnesota and he had gone to a college where they were anti-Semitic, but he was a college guy and they all loved him. Well, he listened to me defending myself and others, and he said, "Now, I just want to tell you something. I went to college and I was beaten up by members of the team and I had won every record there was. But they broke my shoulder. I think that what Lippy was saying" —Lippy was my name at that time— "I feel the same thing. I went and beat the shit out of the guys that did it to me and they stopped doing it." Now in the meantime, because he had changed from being, they thought, a bad guy, that he was the right thing to be with. Now I was –we were just Americans. We didn't know everything about all over the world, but the point was that they changed and within one month, I was already okay.

Now that's a true story.

STAN

I want to get back to your acting career. So eventually you got out here to Hollywood and you were doing movies. On a movie like *Prizzi's Honor* how did you prepare to be that character?

JOHN

Well, as I told you, I was fifty years old when I got to work in Hollywood, and I did not like it. Later on, I got to understand what it was, that there were many people that I did not know. But once I got over that and began to work a lot, and by that time, I was beginning to get great shows on Broadway, that those things were useful for me. And film came along the same way. If a good film came along, and I was in it and I fit right in it, I didn't try to be phony, I was just myself. I found different ways of doing it. By this time, you got to realize, if you've been unemployed for fifty, till you're fifty years old, and believe me, if you can't say anything, then there's something wrong with you.

STAN

So you had plenty of preparation for film work in Hollywood.

JOHN

I went right to it, even if I didn't know what was gonna come along next.

STAN

What kind of a part would you like to play these days?

JOHN

Well, I think the ones that I like, the shows that I like, the actors, the characters. That's the only thing that really excited me and I did the best I could, I did a lot of good shows but not in a....

STAN

But today, would you have liked to have been, say a Moses, like Charlton Heston?

JOHN

I'm sorry you mentioned Charlton Heston.

STAN

Oh, sorry – I won't mention him…

JOHN

That's okay. I think he was not that great an actor. He did at that time, when I came here, was a big shot. Later on, as he went on, he was not that hot anymore. I knew him, I worked for him. We acted in a movie [*Number One,* by David Moessinger (1969)] and he was a famous football player[Ron Catlan, starting quarterback of the *New Orleans Saints*]….I played his coach.

STAN

Oh, really?

JOHN

And he didn't know that….

STAN

John, you're a straight forward kind of guy.

JOHN

I learned, I had learned before he talked.

STAN

The past is the past. In other words, you are a progressive guy, who's here and now – you don't rest on your laurels of yesterday.

JOHN

No. I did not.

STAN
You did a radio show, which I wish I could have seen.

JOHN
You'll hear it. I'll get a copy for you.

STAN
You know, our time has suddenly disappeared…All I can say is, my great guest, Mr. John Randolph, is part of history. So, if you see his movies, you've got it right from the horse's mouth. John, anything to add?

JOHN
Well, I'm telling you truth. I didn't want to come here for any other reason except That. Whatever we talked about. Now nobody here [in studio] listening to us knew that we planned any of this.

STAN
Well, we didn't plan.

JOHN
I think I'm excited enough and joyful to be able to talk where there are Americans. And I'm like they are—and it never occurred to me that with the show you were talking about – I played a character who was a guy who was brought into the whole field of Nazis and everything else, that was stirring up in the United States, now. And that we talked – and some areas, and the KKK, and so forth. I played a man who was fifty years old who thought he had escaped from the Nazis – he took a different name – he was a Jewish guy who was hidden – he kept a different name…

STAN
Folks, all I can say is John Randolph's history is a significant part of our history. Thank you, Mr. Randolph, for sharing it with us.

Marsha Hunt

Chapter Twelve

THE STANLEY DYRECTOR SHOW

Today's Guest
MARSHA HUNT
Actress/Author

July 6, 2012

STAN

My guest, Miss Marsha Hunt, star of Broadway stage, motion pictures, radio… has written books. She has done it all: the movie *Cry Havoc*. How could I ever forget television? *Star Trek: The Next Generation*, *Matlock*, *Murder She Wrote*...

Johnny Got His Gun was a film. Dalton Trumbo wrote that film. That was quite a movie, a very powerful piece of work, yes, and *The Human Comedy*. I saw that film at the Loew's Pitkin in Brooklyn. I believe you are a New Yorker, are you not, Miss Hunt?

MARSHA

Until I came out here.

STAN

You were living in Manhattan?

MARSHA

I was on Broadway when I was seventeen.

STAN

Joy to the World, was that your first Broadway show?

MARSHA

The very first. You've done good research.

STAN

I try. Did you have the jitters going up there, Broadway, going to read for a part? Were you nervous?

MARSHA

I was seventeen when I began in motion pictures. I made fifty movies before I ever did a play – and the first play I ever did was on Broadway. It was a great way to break in to live theatre and to be the star no less my first time up.

STAN

With such elegance and grace.

MARSHA

I was terrified. John Houseman was the producer of that play and I begged him not to star me. He said 'Marsha, you'll have a novelty career.'

STAN

So he was a great booster for you.

MARSHA

In that respect, yes.

STAN

Okay let's talk about the Blacklist a little. Please, you said you had some comments about it.

MARSHA

I don't want to go into it because it was so painful at times. Because it could happen, therefore, could happen again. I do agree to speak one more time on it. But I pretty much told my own tale, but I would like to tell you something that may not be recognized, but that's the story of John Henry Faulk. Is that a familiar name?

STAN

It's a familiar name but you'll have to refresh my memory.

MARSHA

Good. Then it needs refreshing. John Henry Faulk was a
Texan with a wonderful down-home accent who was a comedian,
philosopher, on radio, so popular, that he had his own daily show,
I believe on CBS network radio, and his name appeared in *Red
Channels* and he was promptly dropped by the network sponsor and
he was off the air. John Henry was the one person I know of who
sued about that for libel. He sued *Counter-attack*, the unofficial
right wing pamphlet that didn't quite dare call 150 names listed,
not quite being called communists because they would be libelous,
but hinted that they were well known travelers and sympathetic to
known communists, and therefore not worthy of being on radio
and television. *Red Channels* tackled the motion picture business,
but John Henry fought back, and he hired probably the most
expensive lawyer to represent him and it cost him his career, his
good name, his life savings, his marriage, and anything else you
could name and he won.

STAN

That's a heavy price to pay.

MARSHA

He won after six years. Other people, when he ran out of
money, were sympathetic to his cause and his courage. He told me
Edward R. Murrow kicked in ten-thousand dollars and said "this
is my fight, too." We're all in this with you for Freedom of Speech.
John Henry is the one that I –friends brought him over for dinner
one night – I remember laughing so hard. I so enjoyed him and
so admired him and never thought I would see him again, and I
did in 1989, when there was a festival of movies at the University
of Virginia which decided to feature the blacklist as a topic of the
festival, and invited me and John Henry Faulk among others. Pete
Seeger was invited to be on the panel but missed it as he was ill
and couldn't be there, but John Henry was. It was such a reunion
and was as warm as fellow victims can be. And we were together

every bit of the time, during the festival. I remember at the airport when we were all heading home after the festival was over, talking right up until one of our flights was called. He had such a mission and such intensity about the purpose the blacklisting had given his whole life; by the way, by the time he won his case – the jury awarded him double what he was suing for because they were so enraged. They learned about how he'd been treated, that the trouble was the man he was suing, who was the head of a chain of markets, in upper New York State, who had backed, financed the publication of Red Channels, died of a heart attack and John Henry swore it was nothing but spite, he died sooner than pay, but what he did get was a mission for the rest of his life—and he traveled the countryside like Paul Revere, eloquently warning any audience who would listen, "pay attention, you will lose it if you don't keep track of your freedoms." He memorized the Bill of Rights, the Constitution, the Declaration of Independence, and quoted audiences by the yard, saying, "if you don't defend it you will lose it;" he was amazing. He was so eloquent and so intense; he developed cancer and could only do his speaking between chemo sessions which were debilitating and painful. He died not too long after that film festival, after our reunion, but he wanted me to know, as we visited there at the airport, was the following: "You may have wondered why all this fuss about communism, why it was never outlawed, it was just made the dirty word of all things became worse than rape or murder in American culture, the communist was the enemy." He said, "I finally discovered that was the red flag, the scare with the people who conducted these hearings and these frightening investigations. Communism was not the point, the point was control, and if you could scare the public enough about being associated with, or suspected of communist leanings or membership, anything vaguely that far to the left, you would be frightened into silence—and that meant conformity, that meant you would never question authority, you would never dissent, you would never raise your voice to object to anything, you would go quietly and that would be the battle won, the war won, if you could frighten the public into timidity and acquiescence." They wanted control. That answered something that puzzled me all the years during the blacklist. Why was this blanketing the nation? It started with the movie hearings in Washington, but it spread so rapidly to the other media from movies to radio to TV, and then to information, to the print world of newspapers and magazines, to education to colleges, high schools, and even teachers in grade schools and even to religion. There were clergymen who lost their posts because they sounded too far left and they might be commies. It swept the land into a state of timidity and silence. That was the danger.

STAN

You said a phrase earlier about paying attention. I forget exactly where but there is a line in Arthur Miller's *Death of a Salesman*, "… attention must be paid."

MARSHA

That line is so famous I knew in advance what you were going to say. Attention must be paid.

STAN

Yes.

MARSHA

That was John Henry, like Paul Revere, he went around the country saying "paying attention, or you'll lose it, keep track, defend your freedom of speech, of objection, of questioning because that's the right they fought for and won for us, don't lose it."

STAN

I believe Arthur Miller obviously was influenced greatly by John Henry. There's a starting point to something and Arthur Miller knew him, didn't he?

MARSHA

They could have been keenly aware of each other, but I have no knowledge of that. But I think John Henry Faulk deserves his name to be remembered – and by the way, the state of Texas declared John Henry Faulk Day in his honor.

STAN

Oh, really?

MARSHA

Yes, he was belatedly honored and celebrated. It was a heroic stand that he took and he was speaking for all of us. I want his name and his discovery of what he told me, control, the enemy is control.

STAN

And to think I remember that at one time the Communist Party was on the ballot along with the Socialist Party.

MARSHA

Yes and perfectly legal along with the Prohibition Party. Remember that?

STAN

Well, not quite.

MARSHA

You're not old enough.

STAN

The Liberal Party I remember, but that's amazing. You've shed some light. My book is called *Shedding Light on the Hollywood Blacklist*.

MARSHA

Your title is the Hollywood Blacklist, which is where of course where it began –but the main point is how rapidly it spread. Hollywood was the first target because it was the easiest access to headlines. Everybody knew the name Hollywood and knew those famous people who made movies and that got headlines for rather obscure congressmen on a committee called HUAC.

STAN

That obscure man was Joseph McCarthy.

MARSHA

He was a Senator. It was a House Committee. I didn't know that Joe McCarthy in the Senate ever approached Hollywood, but in fact he seems to have done that and if you're interested in research you might find out when he was here and held hearings. I was not aware of those.

STAN

Maybe it was Martin Dies, the Dies Committee. That started much of what had occurred in Hollywood. I believe that was in 1947.

MARSHA

Oh, in 1947 it was HUAC and chaired by J. Parnell Thomas. I'm sure you have in your book from someone the wonderful tidings that this terrible, gavel-pounding authoritarian chairman of the HUAC committee wound up serving time in a Federal penitentiary where also some of the Hollywood writers he had condemned to prison for defending their rights. J. Parnell Thomas was convicted of bribery or dishonesty. The writers who were cited for "Contempt of Congress," it was contempt of the ethics of a congressional committee they were guilty of and the Supreme Court upheld that charge and they all went off to prison.

STAN

The Supreme Court didn't even consider that it was a First Amendment right.

MARSHA

That's right. When I flew to Washington to protest all this, we were named the "Committee for the First Amendment." The name of our chartered flight to protest what they were doing in Washington, depriving the *"Hollywood 19"* shrank down to the *Hollywood Ten.* Nineteen writers had been called to the witness stand but there were nineteen writers in the first place. The Hollywood 19 was whittled down to ten. Yes, it was recessed after only <u>ten</u> had been heard. We Hollywood protestors who flew to call attention to accentuate the positive about Hollywood movies and somehow tried to fight back against the scary negative headlines: *Hollywood Riddled with Reds*. It dominated every newscast, every newsreel, and every newspaper and magazine, and it just somehow took over the news headlines, *Hollywood Reds*. It was that it wasn't safe to go to movies because you were subliminally being brainwashed and would become disloyal.

STAN

What nonsense.

MARSHA

At stake, Hollywood's good name and the box office and the health of the box office as much as the rights of the Hollywood 19.

STAN

That is like a bad dream to me to go against freedom of speech, freedom of thought, to be an American. They were fascists. I can feel your passion, Marsha, it's refreshing. I love to feel that passion.

MARSHA

That was the reason. I didn't know anything about communism. I was a very busy actress making about six movies a year. I was a political innocent. I simply knew that my industry was under attack and some of the best writers in the business were being badly treated by of all things, by a committee of Congress, and they had to be scolded for that and we had to speak up for our industry and the rights of those writers, and most of all the fear of censorship. That's why the studio heads buckled under.

STAN

As a little story, Abe Polonsky told me that he made more money being blacklisted than he did when he was known.

MARSHA

How did that happen?

STAN

Suppose notoriety. He got so many jobs – and used so many fronts—and that he paid his fronts' income tax, so I think he's quite a guy.

MARSHA

Oh. He worked for it. He sold more scripts.

STAN

Abe would say that with a sly grin when I brought it up. I said, "Gee, after *Body and Soul*, you had to be commercial." I'd say something like, "the studios wanted you to write more scripts." He said he didn't care for being a studio commodity. " A Hollywood writer." He said it with disdain. He was very prideful in not being a hack as a writer. He was an artist.

MARSHA

Oh, I would think he probably was. Well, that is really the tale I had to tell. I wanted attention called to John Henry Faulk. Such a gallant heroic man, John Henry Faulk.

STAN

I'm glad you gave me the opportunity to talk to you, Marsha. John Henry Faulk shall continue living on in books and in documentaries.

MARSHA

He was a true patriot.

STAN

I'm pleased to know. It's a big chapter to me.

MARSHA

I'm so happy to have encountered him on those two occasions and am greatly enriched having known him.

STAN

I'm going to read more on John Henry Faulk.

MARSHA

There was a movie made of him. I believe it was called *Fear on* Trial, directed by Lamont Johnson, a dear friend of mine. William Devane played John Henry Faulk and George C. Scott played the expensive lawyer. It was a fine film. I'm not sure of the title.

STAN

I will Google it and find out about that. [Marsha was correct]

MARSHA

That's the story of John Henry – the motion picture about his struggle.

STAN

What a stellar cast, William Devane and the great George C. Scott.

MARSHA

He was a fine actor.

STAN

You weren't so bad yourself. You were a damn good actress. I watch your movies all the time on Turner Classic. Your eloquence is there, and your class is obvious, I hope you don't mind my being fresh, you're a very attractive woman. I wish I knew you much better.

MARSHA

I wish you the very greatest success because it is a tale that needs getting through to people.

STAN

Thank you so much for your kind words and your participation in this book.

Epilogue

I recently sat comfortably in a chair and read, impatiently, a long list—retrieved from the archive of the Writers Guild of America/ West—of the credits restored to blacklisted screenwriters. The process of restoring those credits began in the 1980s (almost forty years after the blacklist began) and continued at least through 2011. I noted, with some degree of satisfaction, that some of those to whom screen credits were restored had been guests on my cable TV show and I reflected, with sadness, that many of those guests have since died. While I am glad to know that the wrongs committed have been acknowledged and to some extent rectified, I still am not satisfied that the acknowledgment these victims of the blacklist received so late in life amounts to justice. It also grates on one's nerves to realize, in hindsight of course, that some of the things done during the blacklist were just stupid. As noted in a *Los Angeles Times* article in 1997, the Oscar for the script of *The Bridge on the River Kwai*, actually written by blacklisted writers Carl Foreman and Michael Wilson, went to the French novelist Pierre Boulle, who then could neither read nor write English. And as the *Los Angeles Times* writer noted,

Foreman died two weeks after he was told he would finally receive a screen credit and an Oscar, and Wilson was already dead.

While many people may be familiar with the story of the Hollywood Ten, there were many more writers, producers, actors, and directors whose names are largely unknown who suffered the consequences of the blacklist. Let us add to the equation, moreover, that prior to the restoration of these credits, many writers, actors, producers, and directors were either deceased or so physically and/or mentally incapacitated that they could not meaningfully know about, accept, or even reject their prizes of restoration.

The first question one must ask is, "how can you really make such a wrong right?" Taking away years of employment and pride from craftspeople who often struggled for years, going through the hoops and hurdles that one has to go through, to get to be employed in the business in the first place is a terrible thing. After interviewing a number of blacklisted people, and spending time in their company, I learned many more details about how long the sting of past injustices could continue to cause suffering. The band-aid applied to the wounds, the restoration of their own credits, I believe constituted only a quick fix. It took fifty years for their own unions [the Screen Actors Guild, the Directors Guild of America, the Writers Guild of America, and the American Federation of Television and Radio Artists] to apologize for not sticking up for them and helping fight back the tyranny of the political witch hunts.

Now that you've read this book, you, perhaps like myself, may have discovered insights into what the blacklist period was about. I'm confident that you will agree that one of the things that should ring out to all of us is that we must always be vigilant and alert to the possibility (maybe probability) of history repeating itself, and to prevent that by speaking out if necessary. In January of 2011, after the Writers Guild restored yet another credit to Dalton Trumbo, one of the Hollywood Ten, WGAW President Chris Keyser said, "It is not in our power to erase the mistakes or the suffering of the past, but we can make amends, we can pledge not to fall prey again to the dangerous power of fear or to the impulse to censor, even if that pledge is really only a hope." I've taken the pledge and I hope you will, too.

Index

CPSIA information can be obtained at www.ICGtesting.com
Printed in the USA
BVOW020426020513

319622BV00004B/7/P